POLITICKING
WHILE FEMALE

Media and Public Affairs

ROBERT MANN, SERIES EDITOR

POLITICKING WHILE FEMALE

THE POLITICAL LIVES OF WOMEN

EDITED BY NICHOLE M. BAUER

LOUISIANA STATE UNIVERSITY PRESS

BATON ROUGE

Published by Louisiana State University Press
www.lsupress.org

LSU Press Paperback Original

DESIGNER: Michelle A. Neustrom
TYPEFACE: Minion Pro

LIBRARY OF CONGRESS CATALOGING-IN-PUBLICATION DATA

Names: Bauer, Nichole M., editor.
Title: Politicking while female : the political lives of women / edited by Nichole M.
    Bauer.
Description: Baton Rouge : Louisiana State University Press, 2020. | Series: Media
    and public affairs | Includes bibliographical references and index.
Identifiers: LCCN 2020016976 (print) | LCCN 2020016977 (ebook) | ISBN 978-
    0-8071-7291-9 (paperback) | ISBN 978-0-8071-7458-6 (pdf) | ISBN 978-0-8071-
    7459-3 (epub)
Subjects: LCSH: Women political candidates—United States. | Women politi-
    cians—United States. | Women—Political activity—United States. | Political
    campaigns—Social aspects—United States.
Classification: LCC HQ1236.5.U6 P657 2020 (print) | LCC HQ1236.5.U6 (ebook) |
    DDC 320.082—dc23
LC record available at https://lccn.loc.gov/2020016976
LC ebook record available at https://lccn.loc.gov/2020016977

CONTENTS

Part IV: Women in Legislative Institutions

ACKNOWLEDGMENTS

An edited volume is always a collaborative achievement, and this volume is no exception. Jenée Slocum originally developed the idea of creating an edited volume of original academic scholarship based on the 2019 John Breaux Symposium, an annual gathering sponsored by the Reilly Center for Media and Public Affairs at LSU. When Jenée came to me with the idea in the summer of 2018, I was more than a little skeptical that I would be able to pull together this project; but Jenée did not waver in her confidence that I could helm the project. I'm indebted to Jenée for her original inspiration for this project and for her support. More broadly, in her role as the director of the Reilly Center, Jenée has made a strategic choice to highlight research on diversity, gender, race, and representation in the center's programming. I know from my experiences at other institutions that research on these topics is often marginalized if not outright overlooked. The support of Jenée and the Reilly Center for the research conducted in this volume, and a variety of programs on women and politics, is truly invaluable. Every scholar should be so lucky as to have someone like Jenée Slocum supporting their intellectual pursuits.

This edited volume is the first such compilation I have spearheaded. Fortunately, I had an experienced and patient colleague, Josh Grimm, to answer many of my nitpicky and anxiety-ridden questions about how to do this gig. Josh always offered thoughtful advice I almost always took. His sage wisdom and unwavering support was a confidence booster, and helped me move this project to completion.

I'm also grateful to my colleagues at LSU's Manship School of Mass Communication and at LSU Press, especially Bob Mann, who edits the Media and Public Affairs series of which this book is a part. Bob was enthusiastic about the project when he first reviewed the proposal, and helped shepherd the project through the review process. I also appreciate the support and guidance of James Long and the rest of the team at LSU

Press. Everyone at the press worked exceptionally hard to ensure a smooth and transparent publication process.

All the contributors to this project participated in the daylong Breaux Symposium. The symposium featured dozens of lawmakers, political practitioners, and academic researchers who came together to discuss women in politics with hundreds of students and community members throughout the day. The engagement of these stakeholders led to rich and robust discussion about the status of women and politics. I'm grateful to everyone who participated in the symposium for their thoughtful insights, pointed questions, and commitment to improving the status of women in politics every day.

My work on this project would not have been possible without the generous support of the Remal Das and Lachmi Devi Bhatia Memorial professorship. I would also like to thank Martin Johnson, the dean of the Manship School, who not only shows a strong commitment to supporting research on women and politics, but also gave me the time and space to complete this project in its final stages. I'm incredibly lucky to have supportive colleagues in two departments, the Manship School of Mass Communication and the Department of Political Science, at LSU.

Finally, I'd like to thank all the women who have run or are running for political office, especially the women who ran in 2018. Without women signing up to run for political office and challenging the patriarchal norms that guide who can (and cannot) participate in politics, this would be a very thin volume. I hope that more women continue to run for political office. While women's representation is at its highest level ever, there is so much more room to grow and enhance the diversity of voices represented in the political system.

POLITICKING
WHILE FEMALE

INTRODUCTION

NICHOLE M. BAUER

The 2016 presidential election was a historic moment in American politics. A major political party for the first time nominated a woman to run at the top of a major party ticket for the presidency. Indeed, Hillary Clinton's candidacy appeared to start a "glass-shattering" moment in American politics as she had the potential to become the first female president after forty-four male presidents. On Election Day, Clinton did not shatter the presidential glass ceiling. In fact, 2016 was a rare election cycle where women did not win any new seats in Congress—women's representation stagnated. Clinton's presidential loss, coupled with the victory of a male opponent who expressed negative and, at times, openly hostile and misogynist views, spurred women to political action through protest, marches, and running for political office.

Immediately following Trump's presidential inauguration, women and male allies staged a Women's March to protest women's political, economic, and social marginalization. The protests included a broad swath of concerned individuals who came together in Washington, DC, in cities across the United States and around the globe (Berry and Chenoweth 2018). The "gender revolution" sparked by the outcome of the 2016 election did not end with the Women's March. The #MeToo movement began a few months later with high-profile men in business, journalism, and entertainment called to account for their years of mistreatment, harassment, and abuse of women in the workplace. And the movement spread to politics. By the end of the summer of 2018, multiple members of Congress resigned over reports of sexual harassment.

In the midst of protest and social activism, women also signed up for campaign training programs, developed fundraising networks, and ran for political office. In the 2018 election, 309 women filed to run in a primary for a House seat—historically, the highest number of female candidates in any election. Women not only ran for political office, but they ran for political office in riskier races. Past research finds that female candidates tend to run in more liberal, more urban, and more diverse districts (Burrell 1994). Candidates such as Lauren Underwood and Katie Porter ran in House districts long represented by Republicans while Ayanna Pressley and Alexandria Ocasio-Cortez challenged Democratic incumbent men in primary elections. The 2018 midterm elections were noteworthy because of the record number of female candidacies but also because of the historic number of women of color who ran for political office. A report by the Center for American Women and Politics, *Unfinished Business,* details the motivations that propelled women to add their names to the ballot. Many women who ran for office did so due to fear, anger, and anxiety stemming from Hillary Clinton's loss and Donald Trump's win in 2016. These motivations both differ from and fit with the conventional reasons why women run for political office. Women tend to run because they are motivated by a pressing policy issue, such as education or gun violence, that they want to remedy through government (Schneider et al. 2016). Many of the women who ran in 2018 were running because of a pressing issue—a looming era with the potential to exacerbate women's underrepresentation pushed women to run for political office.

The women who ran in 2018 came from diverse backgrounds and did not follow the conventional political path for women seeking political office. Women who run for political office tend to start their political careers later in life, after their childbearing years end (Lawless 2012). Women undertake a comprehensive decision-making process through a relationally embedded model that can slow down their entry into the political pipeline (Carroll and Sanbonmatsu 2013). And women tend to work their way, often slowly, up each rung of the political ladder (Maestas et al. 2006). A substantial number of the women who entered the race for the House in 2018 had no previous political experience holding elected office. Certainly, these women had substantial political qualifications, with many having long careers of political advocacy in their communities, such as Deb Haaland and Sharice Davids, who together became the first Native American women elected to Congress, and Rashida Tlaib and Ilhan Omar who won election as the first Muslim women headed to the House. Other women who ran came from backgrounds in the military, such as Amy McGrath,

Chrissy Houlahan, and MJ Hegar, or backgrounds in intelligence including Gina Ortiz Jones and Elissa Slotkin. These backgrounds are atypical of women, in general, and especially atypical of women who enter politics. That so many women ran for office and did so following unconventional political paths for women, not only at the congressional level but in state and local politics as well, holds promise for building a sustainable pipeline of women to run in future elections.

The "pink wave" of the 2018 midterm elections moved women's representation in Congress from 19% to just under 25%. At the state level, women went from holding an average of 25% of seats across state legislatures to holding just under 30%. Of course, there is considerable variation in women's representation across the state legislative chambers. In West Virginia, women hold only 14.2% of seats in the state legislature, but women hold 52% of seats in Nevada's state legislature—making Nevada the only state where the proportion of women in politics mirrors the proportion of women in the legislature. And when it comes to gubernatorial offices, women in 2018 went from holding six to nine seats. Women broke records with their candidacies in 2018. Three states—Iowa, South Dakota, and Maine—elected their first female governor ever.

Indeed, 2018 was a good year for female candidates. But politics is still, very much, a man's game. At the congressional level, 78% of the candidates who ran for a seat were male, even with the record numbers of women who ran. And many of the pathbreaking female candidates from 2018 lost. MJ Hegar and Amy McGrath grabbed the media spotlight with their candidacies in Texas and Kentucky for their compelling backgrounds as female veterans, but ultimately both lost. While women's representation at a rate of just under 25% in the House is a record-breaking level, it is well below gender parity. Twenty states have never had a female governor. And with the exception of Nevada, women's representation is well below parity with men's representation at every level of political office in the United States. Moreover, the vast majority of women who ran for political office in 2018 ran as Democrats. Out of the 123 women who took a seat in Congress at the start of the 2019 legislative term, only 19 did so as Republicans. Women still face a variety of challenges from building support within their political parties, developing effective campaign messages, and overcoming built-in gender biases.

Amid the social and political changes regarding women's roles in public life, the Reilly Center at Louisiana State University convened the annual Breaux Symposium to discuss the status of women in politics. The symposium brought together a diverse set of scholars engaged in cutting-edge research on gender and politics as well as practitioners who work on these very issues. This edited volume emerged out of those discussions. The symposium participants discussed a variety of barriers women encounter in a political system dominated by men, and offer solutions for navigating these obstacles. The daylong event featured discussions ranging from how to decide whether to run for political office to engaging in political activism *without* having your name on the ballot.

The goals of the 2019 Breaux Symposium were threefold. First, the panels highlighted the unique challenges women face in the political system as both candidates and average citizens. Political participation is an inherently masculine endeavor. Indeed, the country excluded women from political participation for the first 140 years of its existence. Second, the event aimed to highlight the unique opportunities available for women to become more engaged in the political system, either as candidates, activists, or just average people. Increasing public discussion about women's marginalization in public life more broadly carves out opportunities for women to take on new leadership roles. The third goal of the symposium was to highlight the advantages that come from improving women's representation. Just having more women in a legislature, for example, leads to more substantive representation of women, people of color, and other marginalized communities.

Existing scholarship on women's political participation as citizens, candidates, and legislators offers tremendous insights about women's political participation during routine political times, but our current political climate is a departure from politics as usual. For example, research by Dolan (2014) and Brooks (2013) offer instructive insights into whether female candidates face bias among voters. And, work by Ondercin (2017) and Huddy, Cassese, and Lizotte (2008) illustrate the ways in which women's political behavior diverges from men's political behavior. While the extant scholarship on gender and politics is vast and comprehensive, there are a number of unanswered questions about the way women behave as citizens and the challenges women face as political candidates. Rapid changes are occurring regarding how women participate in politics, the way citizens see women's role in the political system, and how the public,

NICHOLE M. BAUER

writ large, values women in public spaces. The essays in this volume address the challenges and opportunities facing women in the midst of this "gender revolution."

The organizing structure of the essays in this volume is that they each explore the multiple dimensions of women's political involvement throughout the "political life cycle" of a woman. The life-cycle frame aims to trace the challenges and opportunities facing women as they move up the political ladder from participating as citizens, candidates, and elected officials. Throughout each of these stages, women navigate gendered political spaces. The concept of a political life cycle is based on the idea that women's political marginalization starts early in life and affects how women form political preferences. These early socialization patterns spill over into the decisions women make about whether to run for political office and how they behave as legislators and leaders. Beliefs about women's roles in public life also affect how the electorate, both male and female, make decisions about whether to support female candidates. The life-cycle structure for thinking about a woman's political career offers a useful framework for understanding how women's political experiences as citizens affect their political experiences as candidates and leaders. This volume is certainly not a comprehensive review of all the obstacles women encounter in politics. Nevertheless, it addresses a range of barriers that hinder women's participation.

The essays are organized into three major sections: women's political participation, running for political office, and serving in political office. The contributors make unique theoretical and empirical contributions to the study of gender and politics. Each essay integrates insights from social psychology, social movements, and intersectionality with existing theories in political science about public opinion formation, political socialization, and voter decision-making. The essays forge new ground in identifying when women might face obstacles in politics, due to their status as women operating in largely masculine spaces, and when women might have new opportunities to advance their political status. Take for example how two contributors tackle the question of intersectional political identities. Mary-Kate Lizotte and Danielle Lemi both wrote essays that shed light on questions of intersectionality and political identity. Lizotte's essay centers on how partisan identities, especially the identity of voters as Democratic, intersects with the gender, racial, religious, and social class backgrounds to shape voter decision-making. This essay addresses a long-standing finding in the literature that female voters vote for Democratic candidates (Plutzer and Zipp 1996), but the extant scholarship, as Lizotte notes, has long treated female voters as monolithic voting blocks. Lizotte addresses this assumption to show that while gender is a prevailing political identity for many women it intersects with other political identities, such as race and religion, in politically consequential ways. Lemi's essay approaches the question of intersectionality from a different angle, focusing on whether a bond based on shared identity as racial minorities exists between multiracial female candidates and minority female voters. Lemi's essay advances research on linked fate as well as the gender-affinity literature. Lemi shows that minority women do not necessarily vote for multiracial female candidates simply because they are female and simply because they are minority women. The multiracial identities of female candidates like former presidential contender Senator Kamala Harris can make it more difficult for them to form coalitions in the minority community. Both essays examine the intricacies of political identity and do so in ways that reflect the growing diversity of the electorate.

Political participation, political leadership, and political institutions are all highly gendered, and racialized, spaces dominated by norms of white masculinity (Hawkesworth 2003, Rosenthal 2002, Brown 2014). The gendered-racialized nature of these spaces can create inherent obstacles for women seeking an entry point in the political system (Dittmar 2015, Kanthak and Woon 2015, Stoddard and Preece 2015). The essays in this volume consider how women are shifting the masculinized ethos of political institutions. Jennie Sweet-Cushman identifies how increases in women's representation in state legislatures, specifically the case of Pennsylvania, affects the types of legislation considered in the legislative chamber, and she shows how Democratic and Republican women work together to achieve policy goals. Anna Mahoney, Meghan Kearney, and Carly Shaffer's essay tackles a critical question about how state legislatures are changing their policies in light of the #MeToo movement. The authors collected sexual harassment policies of nearly all state legislative chambers across the United States and analyzed how those policies protect those who may suffer harassment versus how institutions work to protect themselves. Together, these two pieces of scholarship illustrate how increasing women's representation and elevating women's voices can shift the masculinized ethos that guides political institutions. Breaking down the masculine ethos of politics is especially important for making more long-term gains in women's representation.

Methodologically, many of the essays employ original data analyses, and often use original data collections, to engage in rigorous hypothesis testing. The diversity of methodological approaches is a strength of this volume. Sylvia Gonzalez and Nichole Bauer's essay pairs observational data over time from the American National Election Study with an original survey experiment to track how voters use gender and partisan stereotypes. Gender stereotypes and partisan stereotypes have overlapping content for Democratic women but have conflicting content for Republican women—making these constructs particularly tricky to study. The use of an experiment with survey data is a strength of this essay because the strong internal validity of the experiment complements the strong external validity of the observational data. Another essay in the volume that addresses voter decision-making that also uses an innovative research design is Tessa Ditonto and David J. Andersen's contribution, which relies on data from the 2016 Cooperative Congressional Election Study. The authors test whether voters are less likely to vote for down-ballot female candidates when a female candidate is at the top of the ticket. In other words, the authors directly test whether having Hillary Clinton at the top of the Democratic ticket hampered the ability of women to make long-term gains in representation at lower levels of political office. The use of CCES data, a large-scale nationally representative survey, is a strength because Ditonto and Andersen can measure voter decision-making about actual female candidates outside the experimental lab in the context of real-world elections.

Politicking While Female in 2020 and Beyond

The 2020 presidential elections featured an opportunity for women to make headway in breaking through to the White House with six women, at one point, vying for the Democratic Party's nomination. The six women who ran for the Democratic Party's presidential nomination certainly broke records—between Shirley Chisholm and Patsy Mink's candidacies in 1972 and Hillary Clinton's candidacy in 2016 only a handful of women ran for the nomination of the Democratic Party or the Republican Party. Having women on the debate stages throughout the summer and fall of 2019 drew attention to issues that disproportionately affect women, especially women of color, such as the pay gap, family-leave policies, and the maternal mortality rate. Seeing women on a presidential debate stage started the process of normalizing a woman running for the presidency—a process with the potential to have a role-modeling effect on women and girls, as Monica C. Schneider and Mirya Holman's essay discusses. But running for the presidency as a woman did not come without gendered challenges.

Senator Elizabeth Warren was the first woman to announce her bid for the 2020 presidential election, and the day after her announcement *Politico* ran a news article questioning Warren's likability. The article explained that Warren, and any woman who ran for the presidency, would be deemed unlikable by the electorate by virtue of their sex. Likability is rarely considered to be a problem for male candidates. Immediately after Senator Amy Klobuchar announced her candidacy the *New York Times* ran an article detailing her history of being a tough and demanding boss when it came to managing her staff in the Senate. The implication was that Senator Klobuchar was a bad boss and would, therefore, be a bad leader. Other candidates were simply ignored by the media. Among the first two candidates to drop out of the race were two women—Senators Kirsten Gillibrand and Kamala Harris. Among the top reasons Senators Gillibrand and Harris cited for dropping out of the presidential race were the fundraising barriers. Rosalyn Cooperman's essay shows just how difficult fundraising is for political candidates, especially for Republican women who lack the base of support within the party that so often benefits Democratic women. It may be that Democratic women running at the top of the ticket lack a strong base of fundraising support.

The essays in *Politicking While Female* illustrate what it is like to be a woman navigating a space dominated by and designed to accommodate men. Women develop different political identities compared to men, and these differing identities shape how women participate in politics as citizens and candidates. Identifying how women operate in the distinctly male realm of politics is critical to increasing women's representation. While there are more women in political office than at any other time in history, women's representation is still far below gender parity. Improving women's representation provides unparalleled benefits by increasing the descriptive and substantive representation of women (Pitkin 1967, Mansbridge 1999). Moreover, increasing women's voices in political decision-making enhances the legitimacy of democratic institutions in the eyes of all citizens (Clayton, O'Brien, and Piscopo 2019). Gendered obstacles will emerge throughout the life cycle of a woman's political career, and overcoming these obstacles is pivotal to improving women's representation. The essays in *Politicking While Female* offer unique and instructive insights into how to improve women's representation and, ultimately, how to improve the way our democratic institutions function.

References

Berry, Marie, and Erica Chenoweth. 2018. "Who Made the Women's March?" In *The Resistance: The Dawn of the Anti-Trump. Opposition Movement*, ed. David S. Meyer and Sidney Tarrow. Oxford, UK: Oxford University Press.

Brooks, Deborah Jordan. 2013. *He Runs, She Runs*. Princeton, NJ: Princeton University Press.

Brown, Nadia. 2014. *Sisters in the Statehouse: Black Women and Legislative Decision Making*. New York: Oxford University Press.

Burrell, Barbara C. 1994. *A Woman's Place Is in the House*. Ann Arbor: University of Michigan Press.

Carroll, Susan J., and Kira Sanbonmatsu. 2013. *More Women Can Run: Gender and Pathways to the State Legislatures*. New York: Oxford University Press.

Clayton, Amanda, Diana Z. O'Brien, and Jennifer M Piscopo. 2019. "All Male Panels? Representation and Democratic Legitimacy." *American Journal of Political Science* 63 (1): 113–29.

Dittmar, Kelly. 2015. *Navigating Gendered Terrain: Stereotypes and Strategy in Political Campaigns*. Philadelphia: Temple University Press.

Dolan, Kathleen. 2014. *When Does Gender Matter? Women Candidates and Gender Stereotypes in American Elections*. New York: Oxford University Press.

Hawkesworth, Mary. 2003. "Congressional Enactments of Race-Gender: Toward a Theory of Raced-Gendered Institutions." *American Political Science Review* 97 (4): 529–50.

Huddy, Leonie, Erin Cassese, and Mary-Kate Lizotte. 2008. "Gender, Public Opinion, and Political Reasoning." In *Political Women and American Democracy*, ed. Christina Wolbrecht, Karen Beckwith, and Lisa Baldez. New York: Cambridge University Press.

Kanthak, Kristin, and Jonathon Woon. 2015. "Women Don't Run: Election Aversion and Candidate Entry." *American Journal of Political Science* 59 (3): 595–612.

Lawless, Jennifer L. 2012. *Becoming a Candidate: Political Ambition and the Decision to Run for Office*. New York: Cambridge University Press.

Maestas, Cherie D., Sarah A. Fulton, L. Sandy Maisel, and Walter J. Stone. 2006. "When to Risk It? Institutions, Ambition, and the Decision to Run for the U.S. House." *American Political Science Review* 199 (2): 195–208.

Mansbridge, Jane. 1999. "Should Blacks Represent Blacks and Women Represent Women? A Contingent 'Yes.'" *Journal of Politics* 61 (3): 628–57.

Ondercin, Heather L. 2017. "Who Is Responsible for the Gender Gap? The Dynamics of Men's and Women's Democratic Macropartisanship, 1950–2012." *Political Research Quarterly* 70 (4): 749–61.

Pitkin, Hannah. 1967. *The Concept of Representation*. Berkeley: University of California Press.

Plutzer, Eric, and John F. Zipp. 1996. "Identity Politics and Voting for Women Candidates." *Public Opinion Quarterly* 60 (1): 30–57.

Rosenthal, Cindy Simon. 2002. *Women Transforming Congress*. Norman: University of Oklahoma Press.

Schneider, Monica C., Mirya R. Holman, Amanda B. Diekman, and Thomas McAndrew. 2016. "Power, Conflict, and Community: How Gendered Views of Political Power Influence Women's Political Ambition." *Political Psychology* 37 (4): 515–31.

Stoddard, Olga, and Jessica Preece. 2015. "Why Women Don't Run: Experimental Evidence on Gender Differences in Competition Aversion." *Journal of Economic Behavior and Organization* 117: 296–308.

NICHOLE M. BAUER

WOMEN'S POLITICAL PARTICIPATION

WOMEN'S AND MEN'S IDENTITIES AND 2018 VOTE CHOICE

MARY-KATE LIZOTTE

The election of Doug Jones to the US Senate to replace Jeff Sessions in representing Alabama was a big victory for the Democratic Party. African American women's turnout and overwhelming vote choice for Jones was likely a deciding factor in the election (Duster and Tuakli 2017). This single electoral outcome highlights the import of understanding how gender intersects with other identities in politically consequential ways. Black women have been consistently more likely than white women to vote for Democratic candidates and have recently exhibited the highest levels of turnout among any race-gender subgroup in the American population (Dittmar and Carr 2016). In this essay, I examine how race and other identities intersect with sex on Election Day.

Gender differences, often referred to as gender gaps, in vote choice and party identification did not emerge until the 1970s and were not consistent until the 1980s (Huddy, Cassese, and Lizotte 2008; Ondercin 2017). Recent evidence, however, suggests women may have also contributed to the New Deal realignment in substantial ways, meaning that the gender gap in vote choice may have existed at times prior to the 1970s (Corder and Wolbrecht 2016). Existing work finds women are more likely than men to identify with the Democratic Party with a gap historically ranging from 4 to 12%, and to vote for Democratic Party candidates with a gap historically ranging from 6 to 13% (Huddy, Cassese, and Lizotte 2008). These gender gaps are most often calculated as the differences between women's Democratic identification or Democratic vote choice minus men's Democratic identification or Democratic vote choice. The formula below depicts the calculation.

Vote Choice Gender Gap = % of W voted for Democrat
– % of M voted for Democrat

For example, in the 2000 presidential election, 57% of women voted for Al Gore compared to 47% of men, producing a gender gap of 10% (Huddy, Cassese, and Lizotte 2008). Because women have been more likely than men to vote in recent presidential elections (CAWP 19), the gender gap in vote choice and party identification is particularly consequential.

Women's political participation, activism, and vote choice have garnered much attention in recent years. For some political pundits and journalists, the exit-poll data for the 2016 presidential election were surprising. For example, 54% of women voted for Clinton, but 52% of white women voted for Donald Trump. The Women's March of 2017 and subsequent marches have unfortunately reinforced the notion, which led to confusion among pundits and journalists in 2016, that all women are unified in their political views and behavior. Many women were galvanized by the Trump 2016 win to participate in the 2017 Women's March and oppose his conservative agenda. A substantial portion of women, however, continue to support the Republican Party and vote Republican. In the 2018 midterm election, 40% of women voted for Republicans and 59% for Democrats.

Considering how different subsets of women vote will contribute to our understanding of the gender gap in vote choice as well as how other political identities act as crosscutting pressures on women's political behavior. First, I will provide a critical review of prior scholarship on the gender gaps in vote choice and party identification, considering several relevant theories for the existence of these gender gaps. Second, I will provide a descriptive and exploratory analysis of 2018 American National Election Study data to highlight how other identities influence the vote choice of men and women. This descriptive analysis will include a breakdown of these gender gaps among various demographic subgroups, including race/ethnicity, education level, religiosity, marital status, parental status, and income. Recent media coverage of exit-poll data and scholarship showing differences in vote choice between white women and women of color (Dittmar and Carr 2016; Junn 2017) reveal the need to understand how gender interacts with other demographic characteristics. The results indicate that women were significantly more likely than men to vote for the

Democratic House candidate in 2018, except for among blacks and among individuals with low incomes. The results also illustrate the substantial influence of other characteristics on men and women's vote choice; for example, 71.84% of Latinas versus 58.24% of white women voted for the Democratic House candidate. The multivariate analyses show a significant gender gap, with women more likely than men to vote for the Democratic candidate in the 2018 House, Senate, and gubernatorial elections. These analyses also point to the particular significance of race, church attendance, parental status, education, and age for vote choice in 2018.

Prior Research on the Gender Gap

Gender differences in party identification, vote choice, and public opinion are well documented in prior research. In general, women are more likely than men to identify as Democrats, to vote for Democratic candidates, and to have more liberal positions on various but not all policies. There is some disagreement in the literature as to when the gender gap in vote choice began and whether it was men's or women's partisan movement that caused the gap to emerge (Kaufmann and Petrocik 1999; Ondercin 2017). Opinions differ on several policies with consistent and significant gaps on the use of force, on social welfare issues such as spending on the poor, on environmental policy, abortion, race-related issues, and gay rights, as well as government spending and regulations to protect the environment (Haider-Markel and Joslyn 2008; Howell and Day 2000; Lizotte 2015; Norrander 2008). These various issue gaps contribute to the gap in party identification and vote choice (Chaney, Alvarez, and Nagler 1998; Kaufmann 2002).

THEORIES EXPLAINING THE ORIGINS OF THE GENDER GAP

There are a number of theories as to why on average women differ from men on their party identification, vote choice, and issue positions. First, value differences, such as differences in the endorsement of egalitarianism and humanitarianism, is an explanation with some support. Women's greater propensity to support equality and care for the well-being of others may attract them to the Democratic Party, which is known for advocating for equal rights and for policies that provide for the welfare of citizens. Much of the research on this explanation is limited to public opinion gaps.

For example, humanitarianism partially explains the gender gap in support for the Affordable Care Act (Lizotte 2016). Egalitarianism explains a portion of the gaps on social welfare issues, gun control, proper government role, and racial attitudes (Howell and Day 2000).

Second, prior research has investigated feminism as an explanation for the gap. Feminists are more likely to oppose war and defense spending while also supporting increased social welfare spending (Conover 1988). Thus, feminists may also be more likely to identify as Democrats and vote for Democratic candidates because of the association of the Democratic Party with lower defense spending and higher social welfare spending. Other research on this explanation has argued that independent women, psychologically and/or economically independent, are more likely to vote for Democratic candidates and are likely to be feminists. In the 1980 and 1982 elections, economically independent women contributed to the gender gap in presidential vote choice and the gap in presidential approval ratings (Carroll 1988), but other research does not find this relationship in other presidential elections (Huddy, Cassese, and Lizotte 2008).

Third, political scientists have investigated women's economic marginalization as an explanation. Women are more likely than men to live in poverty and struggle financially (Kimenyi and Mbaku 1995). Economically marginalized women may be attracted to the policy positions of the Democratic Party, which seeks to raise the minimum wage, lower levels of economic inequality, and maintain the social safety net. There is a correlation between the percentage of economically marginalized women and the size of the gender gap in party identification in the aggregate according to time series analyses (Box-Steffensmeier, De Boef, and Lin 2004). On an individual level, low-income women do not appear to substantially explain the gender gap in presidential vote choice (Huddy, Cassese and Lizotte 2008).

Other theories have received less empirical attention but still may provide insight into the gender gap. Women may be attracted to the Democratic Party because of the symbolic images of the political parties, including the gender composition of the parties' congressional delegations (Ondercin 2017). Another possible explanation is that gender differences in issue positions have produced the gender gap in party identification and vote choice. From 1988 to 2000, various issues, including reproductive rights, gender equality, gay rights, social welfare attitudes, racial attitudes, and defense attitudes, have been predictive of party identification for

MARY-KATE LIZOTTE

women and men, but reproductive rights, gender equality, gay rights, and social welfare attitudes have been more determinant for women while defense attitudes decreased in its influence on women's partisanship during this time period (Kaufmann 2002).

Crosscutting Political Identities, Gender, and Vote Choice

Other identities and characteristics such as race, ethnicity, educational attainment, household income, religiosity, parental status, and marital status in addition to gender also influence vote choice. Existing research and polling data provide evidence that gender interacts with these other identities in politically consequential ways. Voter race is an important predictor of vote choice. Democratic Party presidential candidates have not won the White House with a majority of white voters, in the last half-century, instead relying on the black vote to win (Abramowitz 2010). The 2008 presidential election also saw an increase in support of black and of Latinx voters for the Democratic Party candidate (Abramowitz 2010). Latinx voters have been more likely to vote for Democratic presidential candidates by a margin of 18 to 44% from 1980 to 2012 (Lopez and Taylor 2012). Race and gender intersect, creating gender gaps among African Americans and Latinx voters. For example, the gender gap in 2016 among African Americans was 12% (CNN 2016). Among Latinx voters, the gender gap in presidential vote choice was 11% in 2012 (Bejarano 2013).

In terms of socioeconomic status, the research is clearer for the relationship between income and vote choice than for education and vote choice. Individuals with higher incomes are more likely to identify as Republican (McCarty, Poole, and Rosenthal 2006). The gap in vote choice between high income and low income has been recorded at 15% in the early 2000s (Gelman, Kenworthy, and Su 2010). Some research has investigated, with mixed results, whether low-income women are causing the gender gap in vote choice (Box-Steffensmeier, De Boef, and Lin 2004; Huddy, Cassese and Lizotte 2008).

Educational attainment has not had a consistent relationship with vote choice. For example, 50% of those with a bachelor's degree voted for Obama compared to 48% voting for Romney (Suls 2016). In 2016, the gap was 8%. With a slight a majority, 52% of those with a bachelor's degree voted for Clinton compared to 44% of those with less than a bachelor's degree (CNN 2016). The education gap also exists for partisanship but appears to be a recent phenomenon, with 53% of college graduates versus only 46% of those with less than a college degree identifying as Democrats (Suls 2016). Gender appears to intersect with education as well; for example, among whites, college-educated women were more likely than college-educated men and more likely than women without college degrees to vote for Clinton in 2016 (CNN 2016).

Religious identification, religiosity, and morality issues have led to notable divisions in the American electorate. Analysis indicates that the religion gap, differences between those with high levels of church attendance and those with lower levels, first appeared in the 1988 presidential election with a gap of 12.8%, where frequent church attendees were much more likely to vote for George H. W. Bush than Michael Dukakis (Olson and Green 2006). In 2004, being "pro-life," supporting traditional marriage, and preferring a candidate with similar religious beliefs all predicted voting for George W. Bush (Guth et al. 2006). In 2008, religious individuals continued their support for the Republican Party candidate for president (Abramowitz 2010). Religious women, particularly white religious women, tend to vote for the Republican Party unlike secular and African American women (Greenberg 2001).

Being a parent appears to have a generally liberalizing effect. In 2008, parents were not more likely to vote for the Republican Presidential ticket despite its emphasis on Sarah Palin as a mother (Elder and Greene 2012). There do appear to be some differential effects of parenthood on men and women. Motherhood has a more extensive and more consistently liberalizing effect than fatherhood (Elder and Greene 2012). In the 2004 presidential election, mothers were also more likely than non-mothers or men, fathers and non-fathers, to vote for the Democratic candidate while fathers did not substantially differ from non-fathers (Elder and Greene 2007). Evidence suggests that these differences between mothers and fathers arise because motherhood is more likely to be a part of a mother's stable identity while fatherhood needs to be primed in order to have political effects (Klar, Madonia, and Schneider 2014).

The marriage gap refers to the greater propensity of married than unmarried individuals to vote for Republican candidates (Weisberg 1987). The marriage gap emerged in 1972 with married individuals identifying as more conservative and more likely to vote Republican (Weisberg 1987).

The gap has varied greatly in size. Single voters in the 1982 congressional election exit polls favored Democrats by 26 points (Plissner 1983). There appears to be a gender gap among married and single individuals with married women and single women being more likely to vote Democratic compared to married men and single men (CNN 2016).

Finally, research on the 2016 election and the gender gap in vote choice demonstrates how gender interacts or intersects with other identities and attitudes in meaningful ways. Intersectionality denotes the interconnection of two or more identities and how the compounded effect of those identities shapes the outcomes and experiences of individuals (Crenshaw 1989). White women were more likely to vote for Trump than for Clinton the 2016 presidential election. The research on 2016 presidential vote choice indicates many factors influenced the vote of Trump supporters, including racial resentment and sexism (Cassese and Holman 2019; Schaffner, MacWilliams, Nteta 2018; Valentino, Wayne, and Oceno 2018). Sexism, racial resentful attitudes, and having a low income were all significant predictors of white women's vote Trump while church attendance, educational level, and authoritarianism were not predictors (Cassese and Barnes 2018). Similarly, analysis including all women, not only white women, finds that sexism, racial resentment, being white, being an evangelical, and being married are correlated with a vote for Trump; these same identities are associated with a vote for Trump among men as well (Setzler and Yanus 2018)

Expectations

Exit-poll results and scholarly work lead to a number of general expectations similar to prior election results. First, there will be a sizeable and significant gender gap. Second, the gender gap will exist across the other characteristics of race, education, income, religiosity, parental status, and marital status. Third, people of color will be more likely than whites to vote Democratic, and women of color will be more likely than white women to vote Democratic. Fourth, college education and lower incomes will lead to greater support for Democratic candidates. Fifth, secular, childless, and single individuals will be more supportive of Democrats than religious, parents, and married individuals, respectively.

Differences in the 2018 midterm election compared to prior elections may exist because particular issues were salient. The national debate over the Affordable Care Act and climate change may lead to a larger gender gap than in previous elections, because prior work shows gender gaps on these issues (Haider-Markel and Joslyn 2008; Lizotte 2016). Attention to minority rights and women's rights because of the Women's March and other responses to the Trump administration may also lead to a more sizeable gender gap as well as greater support among nonwhites for Democratic candidates. Moreover, identity politics received much attention during the 2016 presidential election as well as with respect to the diversity among Democratic candidates running in 2018. This may produce larger differences between women of color and other groups. Given media coverage of the Trump administration's Supreme Court appointees, frequent church attendees may have been more likely to turn out and less likely to vote for Democratic candidates than in prior elections. Finally, a number of issues such as health care and gun control may have been particularly salient among parents, specifically mothers, producing significant differences in vote choice.

Data, Methods, and Variables

Identities and characteristics such as race and religiosity intersect with gender to produce varying-sized gender gaps between men and women of the same subgroup. Furthermore, although women of different racial, ethnic, educational, and other backgrounds differ in their likelihood of voting for Democratic candidates, all women are more likely than their male counterparts to vote for Democratic candidates. The 2018 American National Election Study (ANES) pilot data provide a nationally representative sample clustered according to House of Representatives districts. The 2018 elections are of particular interest because of the high levels of political enthusiasm and activism leading up to Election Day including but not limited to the Women's March, congressional town-hall meeting confrontations regarding the Affordable Care Act, student-led gun-control protests, demonstrations against the Trump travel ban, numerous statewide teacher protests, and the increase in women, including women of color, running for elected office. These phenomena demonstrate a heightened political engagement, particularly on many public policy issues on which there are sizeable and significant gender differences in public opinion. Prior research often utilizes the ANES to examine the gender gap in vote choice, party identification, and public opinion.

My analysis here is primarily descriptive and exploratory. First, cross-tabulations show what percentages of men and women in different subgroups voted for the Democratic candidate in their House of Representatives race. House races were chosen so as to include all respondents who voted. Not all respondents were in a state with a Senate race or a gubernatorial race, and therefore, this would have meant losing a substantial number of observations. Second, I use logistic regression to investigate which of these characteristics is a significant predictor of vote choice, for the House, Senate, and governorship, when all of the characteristics are included together. I include logistic models of all respondents as well as separate models for women's and men's vote choice to investigate the degree to which other identities intersect with gender.

The House candidate vote choice variable is coded 1 for a vote for the Democratic candidate and 0 otherwise. Individuals that did not vote in their House race are coded as missing. The overall count for this variable is 986 votes for the Democrat, 713 votes for the Republican, and 44 votes for another candidate. Respondent gender is based on a question measuring sex: "Are you male or female?"[1]

The race and ethnicity variables are based on a racial self-identification question. Variables for white, black, and Latinx are included. The white variable is coded 1 for self-identification as white and 0 otherwise. The black variable is coded 1 for self-identification as black and 0 otherwise. The Latinx variable is coded 1 for self-identification as Hispanic and 0 for otherwise. Unfortunately, the ANES does not differentiate between Latinx and Hispanic; Latinx is used because of its inclusive nature and its dominant use in recent discourse.

Educational attainment, household income, religiosity, parental status, and marital status are also included. For educational attainment, those with a bachelor's degree or more are coded as 1 and those with less than a bachelor's degree are coded as 0. For household income, individuals reporting a household income up to $29,999 are coded as having a low income while those reporting a household income at or above $70,000 are coded as having a high income (above the median). For religiosity, individuals stating that they attend church once or more a week are coded as religious while those attending less than once a week are coded less religious. There are likely additional important differences between those who attend religious services never or rarely and those who attend monthly, but for space restraints, these are not analyzed. For parental status, those living with children under the age of eighteen are coded as having children and those not living with children are coded as not having children. Regrettably, this is the standard ANES measure; the ANES does include a question gauging parental status. Finally, for marital status, individuals reporting that they are currently married are labeled as married and all others, single, divorced, widowed, and so forth, are coded as not married. Again, distinctions between never been married and divorced are possible but, due to space limitations, are not analyzed.

Results

Overall, the 2018 cross-tabulation results show substantial differences between men and women of different identities and that all women are more likely than men of the same subgroup to vote for the Democratic House candidate. The gender gap in the 2018 House vote according to exit-poll data was 12% with 59% of women and 47% of men voting for the Democratic House candidate (CNN 2018). To place that gap in perspective, the 2016 gender gap in presidential vote choice was 13% with 54% of women and 41% of men voting for Senator Clinton; the House results in 2016 were similar with an 11% gap: 54% of women versus 43% of men voted for the Democratic House candidate (CNN 2016). The 2018 ANES results are a bit larger than the 2018 exit-poll results with a 15.32% gap: 63.72% of women compared to 48.4% of men voted for the Democratic House candidate. Figure 1.1 displays all of the gender gaps for each subgroup. (Each of the gender gaps except for the gap among blacks and among those with low incomes is statistically significant.)

Among the different racial identities, the gender gap varies quite a bit in size. Among whites, the gender gap is close to the exit-poll results with a gap of 12.54%. According the 2018 ANES, 45.7% of white men and 58.24% of white women voted for the Democratic House candidate. The gender gap in the 2016 presidential and House votes were of similar size, but whites were much less likely to vote Democratic in both. In the 2016 presidential election only 31% of white men and only 43% of white women voted for Clinton while 33% of white men and 43% of white men voted for the Democratic House candidate that year (CNN 2016). The gender gap in vote choice is much smaller and not statistically significant among black voters; 94.62% of black women and 90.48% of black men voted for the Democratic House candidate, resulting in a 4.14% gap. This is much smaller than the 2016 gender gap among black voters, which was 13% in House elections and 12% in the presidential election. The difference between 2016 and 2018 looks to be largely driven by black men who were less likely to vote Democratic in 2016 compared to 2018; for example, 82% of black men voted for Clinton, and 81% voted for the Democratic House candidate in 2016 (CNN 2016). The gender gap is largest among Latinx, with an almost 20-point gap: 52% of Latinos and 71.23% of Latinas voted for the Democratic candidate. This is a much larger gap than in the 2016 election, where the Latinx gap was 6 points in the presidential and House races with 63% of Latinos and 69% of Latinas voting Democratic in both elections (CNN 2016). There are large differences between racial/ethnic groups, with blacks much more likely than whites and also more likely than Latinx to vote for the Democratic House candidate. Black men, for instance, are more likely than white women and Latinas to vote for the Democratic candidate by 32.24% and 19.25%, respectively. Racial and ethnic differences are comparable or larger than gender differences.

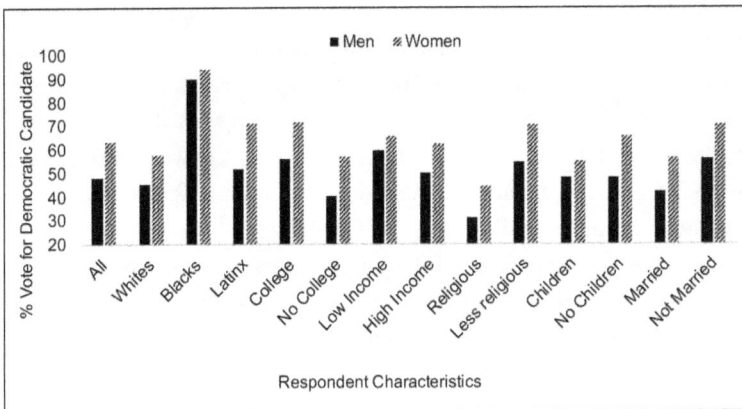

Figure 1.1. 2018 Midterm House Vote Choice Cross-Tabulations

Note: Data from American National Election Study 2018 pilot study. Percentages from cross-tabulations. X-axis is respondent characteristics, and Y-axis is percentage of vote for Democratic House candidate.

Turning to socioeconomic status indicators, men and women of the same educational attainment and household income appear to differ in their likelihood to vote for the Democratic candidate. The gender gap among those with a college degree is 15.42%: 71.84% of women compared to 56.42% of men with a bachelor's degree voted for the Democratic House candidate. Among men and women with less than a college degree, the gap is 16.48 points. Women without a college degree are similar to men with a college degree: 57.25% compared to 56.42% voted for the Democratic in their House race. Only 40.77% of men with less than a college degree voted for the Democratic candidate. Income appears to differentiate the vote of men more so than women. The percentage of low-income and high-income women who voted for the Democratic candidate is similar, 65.75% and 62.73%, respectively. For men, there is more of a difference between those with a low income and those with high income, 59.84% versus 50.42%. The gap is 5.91 points among men and women with incomes below $30,000 while it is 12.31 points among men and women with above-median incomes of $70,000 or more.

Religiosity is an identity that clearly distinguishes between Democratic and non-Democratic voting tendencies. Those who attend church less than once a week are much more likely to vote for the Democratic House candidate than those who attend church once a week or more. Women in both religiosity subgroups, however, are more likely than men to vote for the Democrat running for the House seat. The gap among frequent church attendees is 13.37% with 44.62% of religious women and 31.25% of religious men voting for the Democratic candidate in 2018. The gap is 16.23 points among less frequent church attendees; 71.15% of women compared to 54.92% of men who attend church less than once a week voted for the Democratic House candidate.

Parental status and marital status also appear to influence vote choice and the gender gap. Having children does not appear to influence men's vote choice, with 48.32% of fathers and 48.42% of non-fathers voting for the Democratic House candidate in 2018. Mothers differ from non-mothers with 55.33% of mothers compared to 65.98% of non-mothers voting for the Democratic candidate. This results in a larger gap of 17.56 points among childless men and women compared to a gap of 7.01 points among parents. Non-married individuals are more likely than currently married individuals to vote for the Democratic candidate, with women more likely than men of same marital status to vote for the Democrat. The gap among married individuals is 14.16%, with 42.40% of married men and 56.56% of married women voting for the Democratic candidate. The gap among individuals not married is 14.54%, but both men and women who are not married are more likely to vote for the Democratic House candidate, 56.37% and 70.91%, respectively.

In the logistic regression results, the gender gap is significant in the House, Senate, and gubernatorial analysis. For each type of race, full models as well as separate models including women only and men only are included in table 1.1. The analysis displayed in the table also controls for age and region. African Americans and those with a four-year college degree are consistently more likely to vote for the Democratic candidate in all types of elections as well as in the full models and the separate analyses for women and men. Being white is only marginally significant in two models. White people are less likely to vote for a Democratic senatorial candidate, and white women are less likely to vote for the Democratic House candidate. Frequent church attendees, parents, and older individuals are less likely to vote for the Democratic candidate in House, Senate, and governor races. Motherhood has a more consistent effect than fatherhood when looking at the women-only and men-only models. The effect of age is not significant in the women-only models but is significant in the men-only analyses. White people and those currently married are less likely to vote for the Democratic Senate candidate while the Latinx are more likely to vote for Democratic gubernatorial candidates. Neither of these variables is significant in the women-only or men-only models. Those living in the South are less likely to vote for Democratic candidates in House and governor races, with living in the South significant in the women-only gubernatorial model. Income is not significant in any of the models. In analysis not shown, including the low-income variable instead of the high-income variable or both income variables, does not change the results; income is not significant in any of the models. Again in analysis not shown, including party identification reduces the effect of age and region in the House model to nonsignificance, the effect of being white, being black, church attendance, and age to nonsignificance, and the effect of being female, being Latinx, having children, having a bachelor's degree, age, and region to nonsignificance.

* * *

Table 1.1 Vote Choice in 2018

	House Vote	House Women	House Men	Senate Vote	Senate Women	Senate Men	Governor Vote	Governor Women	Governor Men
Female	0.584 (5.06)**			0.504 (3.88)**			0.534 (4.22)**		
White	-0.373 (1.43)	-0.744 (1.70)+	-0.168 (0.49)	-0.566 (1.80)+	-0.630 (1.26)	-0.560 (1.38)	-0.047 (0.17)	-0.422 (0.95)	0.167 (0.42)
Black	2.586 (5.65)**	2.454 (3.60)**	2.563 (4.00)**	1.717 (3.59)**	1.975 (2.70)**	1.388 (2.15)*	2.592 (5.60)**	2.422 (3.68)**	2.626 (3.86)**
Latinx	0.116 (0.35)	0.044 (0.09)	0.066 (0.14)	0.141 (0.36)	0.191 (0.33)	0.109 (0.20)	0.603 (1.70)+	0.572 (1.10)	0.437 (0.85)
Church	-1.123 (8.56)**	-1.237 (6.88)**	-0.992 (5.14)**	-0.972 (6.66)**	-1.134 (5.66)**	-0.815 (3.78)**	-1.074 (7.45)**	-1.129 (5.80)**	-0.982 (4.52)**
Marry	-0.150 (1.18)	-0.170 (0.96)	-0.068 (0.36)	-0.282 (1.95)+	-0.298 (1.49)	-0.197 (0.92)	-0.151 (1.08)	-0.067 (0.35)	-0.168 (0.80)
Parent	-0.488 (3.19)**	-0.616 (2.91)**	-0.331 (1.49)	-0.358 (2.08)*	-0.278 (1.17)	-0.414 (1.64)	-0.397 (2.34)*	-0.431 (1.85)+	-0.303 (1.22)
BA	0.822 (6.73)**	0.858 (4.78)**	0.794 (4.67)**	0.681 (4.93)**	0.754 (3.75)**	0.598 (3.09)**	0.583 (4.35)**	0.719 (3.75)**	0.442 (2.31)*

Income	−0.168	−0.252	−0.104	−0.051	−0.093	−0.004	−0.227	−0.219	−0.275
	(1.31)	(1.37)	(0.57)	(0.35)	(0.44)	(0.02)	(1.62)	(1.11)	(1.36)
Age	−0.012	−0.002	−0.024	−0.009	0.003	−0.023	−0.010	−0.001	−0.020
	(2.87)**	(0.28)	(3.89)**	(1.87)+	(0.53)	(3.28)**	(2.21)*	(0.14)	(2.91)**
South	−0.219	−0.225	−0.216	−0.221	−0.152	−0.315	−0.334	−0.333	−0.335
	(1.78)+	(1.30)	(1.21)	(1.55)	(0.75)	(1.53)	(2.42)*	(1.78)+	(1.61)
N	1,534	1,587	824	710	630	538	1,233	673	560
R^2	0.13	0.15	0.11	0.11	0.12	0.08	0.12	0.12	0.10

+ $p < 0.1$.
* $p < 0.05$.
** $p < 0.01$.

Note: American National Election Study data, 2018. All models are logistic regression with vote for Democratic candidate equal to 1 and 0 otherwise.

Conclusion

There are several interesting findings from the 2018 election. First, women differ a great deal across various groups. Black women were the most likely, and frequent church-attending women were the least likely, to vote for a Democratic House candidate. In fact, black women at 94.62% were more than twice as likely compared to weekly church-attending women at 44.62% to vote for the Democratic candidate in the 2018 House races. This is also true of men, who differ in their propensity to vote for the Democratic House candidate quite a bit. Second, the percentage of women in all subgroups that voted Democratic is higher than the percentage of men. And all of these differences are statistically significant except for the gaps among blacks and low-income individuals. Third, these various identities suggest important political cleavages between groups. For example, nonwhites are more likely than whites to vote for the Democratic candidate. In addition, the college-educated and lower-income individuals are more likely to vote for the Democratic House candidate. Religious individuals are much less likely than less religious individuals to vote for a Democratic candidate. Finally, unmarried women and childless women are much more likely to vote for a Democrat in a House race compared to married women, mothers, married men, unmarried men, fathers, and childless men.

Some of these findings are surprising given prior research. Earlier investigations of the effects of motherhood find a predominantly liberalizing effect, particularly on social welfare issues (Elder and Greene 2006; 2007; 2012). This would lead one to expect that mothers would be more likely than childless women to vote for Democratic candidates, but that is not the case according to the cross-tabulations of the 2018 House vote. Also, given the correlation between earning a bachelor's degree and higher earnings, some might think it surprising that having a college degree is associated with higher levels of voting for a Democrat. Perhaps this is because of the increase in individuals from historically marginalized groups earning college degrees or the increase in tolerance occurring among college attendees (Henderson-King and Kaleta 2000).

There are limitations to the current analysis. Investigating vote choice in a single year is useful and can provide insight into how identities intersect in the voting booth, but to get a more comprehensive sense of how gender interacts with other identities, examining multiple election years would be beneficial. Moreover, the cross-tabulations provide suggestive evidence of how different subgroups may differ in their vote choice. Cross-tabulations are limited, though, because it is unclear if each of these identities would be significant predictors of vote choice when all are included in a multivariate analysis. The logistic regression results suggest that several of the identities are important predictors of vote choice. In the logistic regression models, gender, race, church attendance, educational attainment, and having children are all significant. But the gender interactions are not significant in the logistic analyses; it is still possible that these intersectional identities are electorally important, just not statistically significant in the small pilot-study sample.

Future work should not only look at these interacting identities across more election years, but should also investigate to what extent having an increase in women running for office and media attention to women running influenced vote choice among the electorate. Do we see such a large gender gap in 2018 because of this electoral context? In what ways did this electoral context, which also included a large number of women of color running for office as well as media attention on those female candidates of color, influence the vote choice of women of color? It is possible that this electoral context influenced voter turnout and vote choice in very interesting ways that likely benefited the Democratic Party. Moreover, the 2020 presidential election will likely replicate many of the dynamics of the 2016 and 2018 elections. For example, white women will likely continue to be more likely than women of color to vote Republican and will likely vote to reelect President Trump. The majority of white women, however, voted for Democratic House candidates. This could be an indication of a shift or be the consequence of higher turnout among Democratic identifiers. Other subsets of women such as women of color, college-educated women, single women, and childless women will likely continue to be loyal and reliable voters for the Democratic Party.

Women are not a unified voting bloc but rather are influenced, just as men are, by their other identities and characteristics. This is politically consequential for future elections and campaigns. If the Republican Party, which has historically been disadvantaged by the gender gap, wants to attract female voters, it could appeal to them based on some of these other identities and characteristics. The Republican Party has already been successful in appealing to religious women. The Republican Party, however, could do more to increase voter turnout among religious women because women who take a literal view of the Bible are less likely to participate in politics (Cassese and Holman 2016). In the future, the Republican Party could try to attract more married women and mothers. The Democratic Party could also consider strategic changes to enhance its appeal to subsets of women. For example, the Democratic Party could emphasize its positions on public school funding and the childcare tax credit to appeal to more parents and, in particular, mothers.

Identity politics is a central force in current politics and has been for some time. The Democratic Party has been known for championing women's, minority, and LGBTQ rights; thus, identity politics has been a prominent part of its appeal to certain subsets of the population. Although the Republican Party and its candidates have at times been critical of the Democratic Party's focus on identity politics, the GOP and in particular Donald Trump also use identity politics to appeal to voters. For example, Republican and Trump rhetoric about immigration likely attracts xenophobic white voters, and Trump relied on gender stereotypes and his own identity as a man to criticize Hillary Clinton, arguing for his own leadership abilities. Identity politics will likely continue to be a part of elections and political campaigns in the future. Voters' identities are correlated with their vote choice in consequential ways.

Note

1. The survey does include a measure of gender but only asks respondent sex. As prior work demonstrates, gender gap results are stronger when a gender measure is used rather than a measure of respondent sex; it is important to note, however, that sex approximates gender for most people apart from roughly a quarter of people (Bittner and Goodyear-Grant 2017). The 2018 ANES also does not include an "other" category or additional response options for individuals who are nonbinary.

References

Abramowitz, Alan L. 2010. "The 2008 Election: Polarization Continues." In *Controversies in Voting Behavior*, ed. Richard Niemi and Herbert F. Weisberg. Washington, DC: CQ Press.

American National Election Studies (ANES). The ANES 2018 Pilot Study (data-

set). Stanford University and the University of Michigan (producers). www
.electionstudies.org.

Bejarano, Christina E. 2013. *The Latino Gender Gap in U.S. Politics.* New York:
Routledge.

Box-Steffensmeier, Janet M., Suzanna De Boef, and Tse-Min Lin. 2004. "The Dynamics of the Partisan Gender Gap." *American Political Science Review* 98 (3):
515–28.

Carroll, Susan. 1988. "Women's Autonomy and the Gender Gap: 1980 and 1982." In
The Politics of the Gender Gap: The Social Construction of Political Influence,
ed. Carol M. Mueller. Newbury Park, CA: Sage.

Cassese, Erin C., and Mirya R. Holman. 2016. "Religious Beliefs, Gender Consciousness, and Women's Political Participation." *Sex Roles* 75 (9–10): 514–27.

———. 2019. "Playing the Woman Card: Ambivalent Sexism in the 2016 US Presidential Race." *Political Psychology* 40 (1): 55–74.

Cassese, Erin C., and Tiffany D. Barnes. 2018. "Reconciling Sexism and Women's
Support for Republican Candidates: A Look at Gender, Class, and Whiteness
in the 2012 and 2016 Presidential Races." *Political Behavior* 41 (3): 677–700.

CAWP: Center for Women and Politics. 2019. "Gender Differences in Voter Turnout." cawp.rutgers.edu/sites/default/files/resources/genderdiff.pdf (accessed
May 21, 2019).

Chaney, Carole Kennedy, R. Michael Alvarez, and Jonathan Nagler. 1998. "Explaining the Gender Gap in US Presidential Elections, 1980–1992." *Political
Research Quarterly* 51 (2): 311–39.

CNN. 2016. "Election 2016: Exit Polls." CNN.com. www.cnn.com/election/2016
/results/exit-polls/national/president (accessed May 21, 2019).

CNN. 2018. "Election 2018: Exit Polls." CNN.com. www.cnn.com/election/2018
/exit-polls (accessed May 21, 2019).

Conover, Pamela Johnston. 1988. "Feminists and the Gender Gap." *Journal of Politics* 50 (4): 985–1010.

Corder, J. Kevin, and Christina Wolbrecht. 2016. *Counting Women's Ballots.* New
York: Cambridge University Press.

Crenshaw, Kimberlee. 1989. "Demarginalizing the Intersection of Race and Sex:
A Black Feminist Critique of Antidiscrimination Doctrine, Feminist Theory
and Antiracist Politics." *University of Chicago Legal Forum* 1989 (1): 139–67.

Dittmar, Kelly, and Glynda C. Carr. 2016. "Black Women Voters: By the Numbers."
Huffington Post. secure.action.news/newstempch.php?article=/kelly-dittmar
/black-women-voters-by-the_b_9389330.html (accessed May 18, 2019).

Duster, Chandelis R., and Foluké Tuakli. December 13, 2017. "Why black women
voters showed up for Doug Jones." NBC News. www.nbcnews.com/news/nbc
blk/why-black-women-showed-vote-doug-jones-n829411 (accessed May 29,
2018).

Elder, Laurel, and Steven Greene. 2006. "The Children Gap on Social Welfare and the Politicization of American Parents, 1984–2000." *Politics & Gender* 2(4): 451–72.

———. 2007. "The Myth of 'Security Moms' and 'NASCAR Dads': Parenthood, Political Stereotypes, and the 2004 Election." *Social Science Quarterly* 88 (1): 1–19.

———. 2012. "The Politics of Parenthood: Parenthood Effects on Issue Attitudes and Candidate Evaluations in 2008." *American Politics Research* 40 (3): 419–49.

Gelman, Andrew, Lane Kenworthy, and Yu-Sung Su. 2010. "Income Inequality and Partisan Voting in the United States." *Social Science Quarterly* 91 (5): 1203–19.

Greenberg, Anna. 2001. "Race, Religiosity, and the Women's Vote." *Women & Politics* 22 (3): 59–82.

Guth, James L., A. Kellstedt Lyman, Corwin E. Smidt, John C. Green. 2006. "Religious Influences in the 2004 Presidential Election." *Presidential Studies Quarterly* 36 (2): 223–42.

Haider-Markel, Donald P., and Mark R. Joslyn. 2008. "Beliefs about the Origins of Homosexuality and Support for Gay Rights: An Empirical Test of Attribution Theory." *Public Opinion Quarterly* 72 (2): 291–310.

Henderson-King, Donna, and Audra Kaleta. 2000. "Learning About Social Diversity: The Undergraduate Experience and Intergroup Tolerance." *Journal of Higher Education* 71 (2): 142–64.

Howell, Susan E., and Christine L. Day. 2000. "Complexities of the Gender Gap." *Journal of Politics* 62 (3): 858–74.

Huddy, Leonie, Erin Cassese, and Mary-Kate Lizotte. 2008. "Sources of Political Unity and Disunity Among Women: Placing the Gender Gap in Perspective." In *Voting the Gender Gap,* ed. Lois Duke Whitaker. Champaign: University of Illinois Press, 141–69.

Junn, Jane. 2017. "The Trump Majority: White Womanhood and the Making of Female Voters in the US." *Politics, Groups, and Identities* 5 (2): 343–52.

Kaufmann, Karen M. 2002. "Culture Wars, Secular Realignment, and the Gender Gap In Party Identification." *Political Behavior* 24 (3): 283–307.

Kaufmann, Karen M., and John R. Petrocik. 1999. "The Changing Politics of American Men: Understanding the Sources of the Gender Gap." *American Journal of Political Science* 43 (3): 864–87.

Kimenyi, Mwangi S., and John Mukum Mbaku. 1995. "Female Headship, Feminization of Poverty and Welfare." *Southern Economic Journal* 62 (1): 44–52.

Klar, Samara, Heather Madonia, and Monica C. Schneider. 2014. "The Influence of Threatening Parental Primes on Mothers' Versus Fathers' Policy Preferences." *Politics, Groups, and Identities* 2 (4): 607–23.

Lizotte, Mary-Kate. 2015. "The Abortion Attitudes Paradox: Model Specification and Gender Differences." *Journal of Women, Politics & Policy* 36 (1): 22–42.

———. 2016. "Investigating Women's Greater Support of the Affordable Care Act." *Social Science Journal* 53 (2): 209–17.

Lopez, Mark Hugo, and Paul Taylor. 2012. "Latino Voters in the 2012 Election." *Pew Hispanic Center Hispanic Trends.* www.pewresearch.org/hispanic/2012/11/07/latino-voters-in-the-2012-election/ (accessed January 31, 2020).

McCarty, Nolan, Keith T. Poole, and Howard Rosenthal. 2006. *Polarized America: The Dance of Political Ideology and Unequal Riches.* Cambridge, MA: MIT Press.

Norrander, Barbara. 2008. "The History of the Gender Gaps." In *Voting the Gender Gap,* ed. Lois Duke Whitaker. Champaign: University of Illinois Press, 9–32.

Olson, Laura R., and John C. Green. 2006. "The Religion Gap." *PS: Political Science & Politics* 39 (3): 455–59.

Ondercin, Heather L. 2017. "Who Is Responsible for the Gender Gap? The Dynamics of Men's and Women's Democratic Macropartisanship, 1950–2012." *Political Research Quarterly* 70 (4): 749–61.

Plissner, Martin. 1983. "The Marriage Gap." *Public Opinion* 5 (4): 53.

Schaffner, Brian F., Matthew MacWilliams, and Tatishe Nteta. 2018. "Understanding White Polarization in the 2016 Vote for President: The Sobering Role of Racism And Sexism." *Political Science Quarterly* 133 (1): 9–34.

Setzler, Mark, and Alexandra B. Yanus. 2018. "Why Did Women Vote for Donald Trump?" *PS: Political Science & Politics* 51 (3): 523–27.

Suls, Rob. September 15, 2016. "Educational Divide in Vote Preferences on Track to Be Wider than in Recent Elections." Pew Research Center. www.pewresearch.org/fact-tank/2016/09/15/educational-divide-in-vote-preferences-on-track-to-be-wider-than-in-recent-elections/ (accessed May 21, 2019).

Valentino, Nicholas A., Carly Wayne, and Marzia Oceno. 2018. "Mobilizing Sexism: The Interaction of Emotion and Gender Attitudes in the 2016 US Presidential Election." *Public Opinion Quarterly* 82 (S1): 799–821.

Weisberg, Herbert F. 1987. "The Demographics of a New Voting Gap: Marital Differences in American Voting." *Public Opinion Quarterly* 51 (3): 335–43.

CAN ROLE MODELS HELP INCREASE WOMEN'S DESIRE TO RUN?

Evidence from Political Psychology

MONICA C. SCHNEIDER AND MIRYA R. HOLMAN

Secretary Clinton is a role model for all of us.

—KIRSTEN GILLIBRAND, April 9, 2019

Democrats grieved the loss of Hillary Clinton in 2016 because she was their preferred candidate. Gender scholars lamented the loss because it also meant that breaking the "highest, hardest glass ceiling" would have to wait for at least another presidential election cycle. Having people in office who share descriptive characteristics with a group in the population traditionally excluded from politics—or descriptive representation—improves democratic legitimacy and can facilitate a relationship between underrepresented groups and government (Mansbridge 1999; Pitkin 1967). Indeed, women who hold elective office could potentially act as role models to encourage more women to enter political careers; female congresswomen themselves identify one of their functions as inspiration for the next generation (Dittmar, Sanbonmatsu, and Carroll 2018). Political pundits and scholars observing both Clinton's candidacy and the 2018 election, where a number of new Democratic women were elected to the US House of Representatives, speculated about long-term effects of the influx on other women (Jordan 2018; Yglesias 2016; Bonneau and Kanthak 2018; Campbell and Wolbrecht 2019). Given the disparity in the number of women who hold office compared to men (Center for

American Women and Politics 2019), as well as the ambition gap between men and women in their interest in running for and holding public office (Crowder-Meyer 2018; Holman and Schneider 2018; Schneider et al. 2016; Silva and Skulley 2019), such inspiration has significant potential for changing women's representation in American politics.

Does the presence of women in political office increase women's interest in politics and willingness to run for office? Some evidence would suggest yes, especially for girls and younger women (Campbell and Wolbrecht 2006; Alexander 2012; Beauregard 2017; Elder 2004; Wolbrecht and Campbell 2017). Women may be more willing to run for office when other women have already run for that or similar offices (Ladam, Harden, and Windett 2018); such new candidacies may also lead to a more diverse set of women in office (Barnes and Holman 2018, forthcoming; Cargile 2016). In nonpolitical domains, such as science, technology, engineering and math (STEM), identifying with role models and their experiences seems to increase interest in STEM careers (see Lockwood 2006) and improve outcomes in STEM courses (Herrmann et al. 2016). Thus, women as role models have great *potential* to inspire women's interest and motivation for political careers.

Yet, observational research in the political domain has often concluded that female role models have limited influence (Broockman 2014; Gilardi 2015; Wolak 2015). The effects of women lawmakers as role models are inconsistent (Clayton 2015; Zetterberg 2009). Some researchers found that competitive female candidates increased women's political engagement and interest in serving in politics (Alexander 2012; Atkeson 2003; Karp and Banducci 2008; Ladam, Harden, and Windett 2018). Others demonstrate that the effect is stronger for co-partisans and young people (Mariani, Marshall, and Mathews-Schultz 2015; Wolbrecht and Campbell 2007; Bonneau and Kanthak 2018; Wolbrecht and Campbell 2017) and that a role model affected female constituents the first time she was elected in a district, but the impact declined with subsequent female politicians (Broockman 2014; Gilardi 2015; Wolak 2015). Much of this research also examined population-level shifts, with little attention paid to how micro-level individual factors may be shaped (or not) by role models (but see Greenlee, Holman, and VanSickle-Ward 2014; and Bonneau and Kanthak 2018). Such variability in effects warrants a deeper investigation into the mechanisms of role-model effects in political ambition.

Role models are "individuals who provide an example of the kind of success that one may achieve, and often also provide a template of the behaviors that are needed to achieve such success" (Lockwood 2006, 36); they differ from mentors in that mentorship requires a close personal relationship. Role models may affect people because of their mere presence, particularly when someone shares characteristics with the role models, or because of how they behave in a role. Because of the similarities between STEM careers and politics in underrepresentation of women, research on role-model effects in STEM can assist with predictions (O'Brien et al. 2017; Diekman et al. 2017). Such research suggests that role models positively influence women when they share characteristics, such as sex (Lockwood 2006; Stout et al. 2011) and when the women have a general sense of feeling similar to the role model (Lockwood 2006; Hoyt and Simon 2011) and identify with the role model. Identifying with and feeling similar to a role model may help women feel efficacious and inoculate against feelings of isolation (Buunk, Peiró, and Griffioen 2007; Dasgupta 2011; Stout et al. 2011) and improve their sense of belonging in a particular domain (Lockwood 2006; Cheryan et al. 2011; Cheryan, Drury, and Vichayapai 2013).

Role models' presence and behavior might provide insight into the particular benefits of a career. Such insight is important because perceptions of a political career deter women's entry. Men and women alike believe that a political career involves the pursuit of power-related goals, such as status, power, and recognition, as opposed to either independence goals (achievement, individualism, and demonstration of skill) or communal goals (helping and caring for others' needs, serving humanity, and working with people) (Schneider et al. 2016). But these perceptions damage women's ambition for politics far more than men's (Preece and Stoddard 2015a; Schneider et al. 2016) because men and women develop differential career preferences based on the goals that are associated with traditional gender roles (Diekman and Schneider 2010; Schneider and Bos 2019; Diekman et al. 2017; Bakan 1966). This means that women, relative to men, are more likely to express interest in careers when the activities fulfill communal goals, such as helping and working with others, and reject careers that either do not allow the pursuit of these goals or when they overemphasize power-related goals (Diekman et al. 2017; Schneider et al.

2016). Women's lower expressed interest in power-related goals is relatively minor, but together with differences in tolerance for conflict, it mediates the relationship between gender and political ambition (Schneider et al. 2016). Scholars have also found that views of politics as risky or just a general aversion to elections depresses women's ambition (Kanthak and Woon 2015; Sweet-Cushman 2016).

Research on interventions in the STEM context has shown that when describing STEM careers differently—as affording the opportunity to fulfill communal goals—women's interest in STEM careers increased (Diekman et al. 2011; Clark, Fuesting, and Diekman 2016). Prior research has demonstrated this effect in politics with a manipulation describing the day in the life of a politician as communal or power-oriented (Schneider et al. 2016). Instead of using generic descriptions of the career to examine its effects, we examine whether the behavior of a female or male role model engaging in communal activities within the context of a political career positively affects women. In research on STEM, the behavior of the role model influenced interest in STEM regardless of the role model's sex (Fuesting and Diekman 2017); however, given findings that female role models have unique potential in the political domain (Campbell and Wolbrecht 2006; Alexander 2012; Beauregard 2017; Elder 2004; Wolbrecht and Campbell 2017), we suspect that both the sex of the role model and behavior will together have the most influence over inspiring women. In other words, we predict that a female role model would inspire women through an increased sense of identity and similarity because shared sex and her communal behavior would be most likely to persuasively demonstrate aspects of a political career that are consistent with women's goals. Alternatively, women may not feel inspired by the role model if her success seems out of reach (Hoyt and Simon 2011; Hoyt 2013).

Women may observe a role model and determine that she is too dissimilar to be an inspiration (Lawson and Lips 2014; Lockwood 2006; Lockwood and Kunda 1997) or that the specific goals achieved by the role model are unattainable (Pomaki, Karoly, and Maes 2009). For example, extant research found female role models in masculine STEM careers, who acted in a feminine as opposed to a masculine manner, depressed interest because the combination of femininity and success appeared extraordinary especially among girls who expressed a preference for subjects other than those in STEM (Betz and Sekaquaptewa 2012; Richards and Hewstone 2001; see also Rickabaugh 1995 for perceptions of political activists).

To sum up the psychological literature, female role models seem to be better at inspiring women (Lockwood 2006), and describing a career as communal also increases women's interest in it (Diekman et al. 2011). This leads to the prediction that female leaders pursuing communal activities in political office would (more than male leaders or those pursuing power-related activities) serve as the ideal role model to spur the political ambition and identity of like-minded women. However, the particular combination of a female representative who pursues communal activities may be so unusual that it causes women to view her as dissimilar or her success as unattainable (Betz and Sekaquaptewa 2012). We pursue exploratory experimental studies to untangle these disparate predictions.

Methods

Using experimental interventions to understand role-model effects has been a standard approach in psychology and education for decades. Less is known about these kinds of interventions in studies of political ambition (but see Schneider et al. 2016). Thus, our study design mimics those used in reframing STEM careers (Diekman et al. 2011; Clark, Fuesting, and Diekman 2016). While the experimental treatment here is somewhat artificial since career preferences develop over time and in response to a variety of different factors (Lent, Brown, and Hackett 2002), the experimental design sets up a high bar for finding effects on career-preference-dependent variables. Using an experimental design allows us high internal validity to isolate the effects of role-model and career presentation which come from the very real messages that women and men receive about political careers (Holman and Schneider 2018). Finally, we are not the first to isolate effects in the lab that have been shown to have behavioral effects down the line (Landau et al. 2014).

DESIGN

Participants in both studies read a short paragraph about a day in the life of a man or woman in the state legislature from his or her perspective (see below). The treatment varied in its communal or power focus. For example, the communal treatment introduced the leader's goals as, "A career as a politician helps me fulfill my broader goals of helping and caring for others, attending to others' needs, serving my community, and working with people." The communal treatment then goes on to discuss a typical day for the leader, including, "Like most of my colleagues, I keep up to date with any issues affecting constituents by making personal visits and phone calls. After my committee meetings, I have some time to help constituents by assisting them with the bureaucracy; for example, I spend a lot of time making sure veterans receive benefits." The power treatment, on the other hand, begins with the political leader discussing how the political career "helps me fulfill my broader goals of gaining status and recognition and promoting my success" and goes on to detail, "Like most of my colleagues, I am working towards being head of a committee. After my committee meetings, I have some time to privately negotiate with colleagues or members of other political parties in order to reconcile differing interests, if possible."

Sample Experimental Treatments

Power, female representative

The following is a summary of a day in the life of Patricia Johnson, a Representative in the State Legislature. Please read the passage carefully and answer the corresponding questions.

A career as a politician helps me fulfill my broader goals of achieving power, status, self-promotion, and recognition. My day starts with an all staff conference call from the car on the way to my office where we discuss sending out campaign materials with details of my accomplishments and the possibility of crafting a negative ad about my opponent. Most of my day is filled with sitting in committee meetings, where we debate the merits of proposals and bill amendments. Like most of my colleagues, I am working towards being head of a committee. After my committee meetings, I have some time to privately negotiate with colleagues or members of other political parties in order to reconcile differing interests, if possible. Holding office means long and busy days, but going through the public debates with my opponents and raising money from constituents was worth it because I now have a real voice to persuade constituents of the policies that I think will be best for my district.

Communal, male representative

The following is a summary of a day in the life of Tom Johnson, a Representative in the State Legislature. Please read the passage carefully and answer the corresponding questions.

A career as a politician helps me fulfill my broader goals of helping and caring for others, attending to others' needs, serving humanity, and working with people. My day starts with an all staff conference call from the car on the way to my office where we discuss planning several events with constituents, including town hall meetings, parades, and rallies. Most of my day is filled with sitting in committee meetings where I work with a team of lawmakers, constituents, and interest groups to discuss appropriate legislation. Like most of my colleagues, I keep up to date with any issues affecting constituents by making personal visits and phone calls. After my committee meetings, I have some time to help constituents by assisting them with the bureaucracy; for example, I spend a lot of time making sure veterans receive benefits. Holding office means long and busy days, but going door to door meeting with constituents and listening to what issues are important to them was worth it because I now have a real voice to work towards promoting and voting for policies that improve my community.

Both treatments are based on literature on the day-to-day activities of political leaders from two reports about the job descriptions of lawmakers and fall under the categories of legislative/policy work, constituent issues, political campaign work, and press/media relations (Congressional Management Foundation 2013). Of course, politicians engage in both power and communal tasks and cannot limit themselves to one or the other. Politicians do, however, have choices in how they spend their time, how they present themselves, and how aggressive they want to be in pursuing leadership roles within office. Moreover, the perceptions of political life differ vastly from the actuality of political life, as quantitative studies have shown (Schneider et al. 2016).

Study 1 varied the sex (man or woman) and behavior (power or communal career goals) in a 2×2 design. In Study 2, we used a female role model only and varied the power or communal approach. Both studies

MONICA C. SCHNEIDER AND MIRYA R. HOLMAN

included ambition, identity, similarity, and attainability as dependent variables.

Ambition. Political ambition was measured in both studies by three questions used in prior research: "If you have never run for office, have you ever thought about running for office?" "At some point in your life, how likely is it that you would ever run for office?" and "How enjoyable do you think a career as an elected official would be?" (Lawless and Fox 2010; Schneider et al. 2016; Holman and Schneider 2018; Preece and Stoddard 2015a, 2015b). These questions measure *nascent* or early political ambition, which has been found to connect to an actual run for office (Lawless and Fox 2010; Schneider et al. 2016; but see Carroll and Sanbonmatsu 2013). Because the items run on scales of different lengths, we used the single retained factor from a confirmatory factor analysis to create factor scores of ambition. These composite scores are zero-mean centered where positive values indicate higher levels of political ambition.

Identity. We asked respondents to agree or disagree with three statements identifying with the life of or the accomplishments of the representative and admiring the representative to ascertain feelings of closeness between respondent and role model (Hoyt, Burnette, and Innella 2012). We measured agreement on these statements on a five-point scale (Study 1) or a seven-point scale (Study 2) ranging from "Strongly Disagree" to "Strongly Agree."

Similarity. Using the same agreement-scale format, we measured similarity in Study 1 through a single statement, "The state representative and I are very similar," and in Study 2 through the similarity statement and a reverse-coded dissimilar statement, "The state representative and I are very dissimilar" (Lockwood 2006).

Attainability. Attainability captures the respondent's feelings that s/he can accomplish goals similar to those of the role model (Lawson and Lips 2014; Pomaki, Karoly, and Maes 2009) or that the respondent's future self will be similar to the role model (Lockwood 2006). In Study 1, we used agreement or disagreement with four items to ascertain whether a future self could attain the same kind of success: "The state representative has accomplished more in her life than I can hope to," "I will never attain success like that of the state representative," "The state representative's accomplishments are out of reach for me," and "I will obtain a similar level of success in my own career as the state representative has obtained in their career." The first three statements were reverse coded. In Study 2, we used only the first two statements.

Finally, in Study 1 we added a more detailed assessment of attainability by using a battery of six statements specific to performance in a political career: "If I wanted to, I think it would be possible for me to attain the kind of position that the representative has," "It would be difficult to perform well in a position like this," "If I wanted to, I think I would be able to perform well in this position," "It would be difficult to achieve this position," "I have the necessary skills to attain a position like this," and "I have the necessary skills to perform well in the position that the representative has."

For all measures, including ambition, identity, similarity, and attainability, measures are coded so that higher values indicate more of the positive measure, that is, more ambition or attainability.

SAMPLES

Each sample reported was of female respondents, screened to include only citizens, college students, or college graduates, recruited via Amazon.com's Mechanical Turk (MTurk).[1] MTurk's respondents are more representative of Americans than convenience samples, but one critique of MTurk's respondents is that they are more liberal, educated, and politically active than the general public (Berinsky, Huber, and Lenz 2012; Krupnikov and Levine 2014). Our selection of college students and college graduates in addition to these built-in biases give us an appropriate convenience sample from which future candidates are likely to emerge.

Results

In Study 1, we conducted 2 (sex of lawmaker) × 2 (gendered behavior of lawmaker) ANOVAs, an analysis of variance, examining main effects of each independent variable and their interaction. For Study 2, which only used a female representative, we conducted a one-way ANOVA (the equivalent of a difference of means t-test) to compare the communal and power gendered approaches. Results are presented in text and in table 2.1.

Political Ambition: We find little evidence of any effects on political

MONICA C. SCHNEIDER AND MIRYA R. HOLMAN

Table 2.1 Sample Means

	Study 1	Study 2
Role-model sex effects on political ambition	Tom $\bar{x} = -.13$ Patricia $\bar{x} = -.13$ $p = .94$	
Role-model sex and gendered behavior effects on political ambition	Power (Tom) $\bar{x} = -.17$ Communal (Tom) $\bar{x} = -.07$ Power (Patricia) $\bar{x} = -.15$ Communal (Patricia) $\bar{x} = -.11$ p (career goals) $= .32$ p (interaction) $= .73$	Power (Patricia) $\bar{x} = -.02$ Communal (Patricia) $\bar{x} = .11$ $p = .44$
Identification	Power (Tom) $\bar{x} = 2.29$ Communal (Tom) $\bar{x} = 2.95$ Power (Patricia) $\bar{x} = 2.48$ Communal (Patricia) $\bar{x} = 3.12$ p (career goals) $= .00$ p (role model gender) $= .05$ p (interaction) $= .91$	Power (Patricia) $\bar{x} = 2.72$ Communal (Patricia) $\bar{x} = 3.86$ $p = .00$

Note: Analyses were one- or two-way ANOVAs.

ambition, as displayed in table 2.1. In Study 1, manipulating the sex of the role model failed to produce a statistically significant difference on the ambition of our female respondents. The gendered approach of the role model also does not seem to matter; that is, describing the day of a candidate as pursuing communal goals did not improve ambition compared to the day described as pursuing power-related goals. The interaction between the two also failed to meet significance. In short, our expectation that a female role model who pursued communal goals would improve political ambition was not supported; our manipulations did not affect ambition.

Identification: Respondents in Study 1 identified more with the female leader ($\bar{x} = 2.82$) than the male ($\bar{x} = 2.59$), and in both studies female respondents were significantly more likely to identify with the representative who used a communal approach rather than a power approach. However, the interaction between sex and gendered approach was not significant (Study 1).

Similarity: Respondents in Study 1 felt no more similar to the female than to the male leader. A significant main effect of the gendered approach revealed that women felt less similar to the leader in in the power treatment ($\bar{x}$ = 2.07) than in the communal treatment ($\bar{x}$ = 2.48), p = 0.0001. The interaction between leader gender and the power or communal treatment was not significant, p = 0.97. In Study 2, taking a power approach also caused respondents to feel less similar to the leader ($\bar{x}$ = 1.23) compared to when she took a communal approach ($\bar{x}$ = 2.16), p = 0.0004.

Attainability: Women in Study 1 viewed the communal condition as marginally more attainable ($\bar{x}$ = 2.97) than the power condition ($\bar{x}$ = 2.87), p = 0.08, whereas in Study 2, respondents identified the power representative's accomplishments as more attainable ($\bar{x}$ = 3.13) compared to the representative pursuing communal goals ($\bar{x}$ = 2.41), p = 0.012 on a 7-point scale.

Study 1 participants also reported feeling that the state representative's position was more attainable when described as a man ($\bar{x}$ = 3.01) than as a woman ($\bar{x}$ = 2.85), p = 0.01, but the interaction between the representative's sex and approach was not significant. There were no effects of sex or gendered approach on the additional measure of attainability in Study 1 that related to specific political career tasks.

Discussion, Conclusions, and Implications

Our (lack of) findings might suggest that female role models do not directly increase the political ambition of female respondents regardless of their gendered approach. However, such a conclusion may be premature. Other work shows that change in career interest occurs when interactions with a female role model are in-depth (Greenlee, Holman, and VanSickle-Ward 2014), when a female scientist portrays herself as a stereotypical woman in her personal life and approaches her career by pursuing communal goals (Clark, Fuesting, and Diekman 2016), or when there is direct communication from a female role model (Herrmann et al. 2016). Exposure may need to be repeated or more detailed to shape political ambition; in short, a simple paragraph-long intervention may not work. We encourage future scholars to create experimental paradigms that utilize fuller manipulations.

Our findings on identification and similarity demonstrate some promise. Women identified with the female role model more than with the male, and the role model with the communal approach over the power approach, regardless of the role model's sex. We did not, however, find that these changes influenced political ambition, nor did we find anticipated interactions between sex and gendered approach. Still, the consistent finding that a gendered approach increases women's feelings of similarity and identification with a political representative could be substantively important, especially as repeated exposure to role models in the real-world setting accumulates over time. Moreover, our measures of political ambition may not have the sensitivity to detect small changes in ambition in the experimental setting since the questions were designed to measure nascent political ambition as a largely stable construct (Lawless and Fox 2010). We anticipate the development of newer measures of political ambition along with a reconceptualization of political ambition as an ever-changing construct (Shames 2017; Sweet-Cushman 2018) to understand how changes in identity and similarity might produce long-term effects on ambition.

Our findings on attainability, however, were inconclusive. Female respondents did not consistently respond to either the communal or the power approach as more or less attainable. Nor was there an interaction between the sex of the representative and the gendered approach on attainability. There may be individual-level factors unaccounted for in our study that affect whether women who view a communal or a power approach consider it to be an attainable feat. Future research might explore such moderators.

Our findings also do not account for the importance of intersectional identities in shaping attitudes about the political system (McCall 2005; Farris and Holman 2014; Brown 2014a, 2014b; Lizotte 2020). Previous work demonstrates the importance of considering how gender and race and ethnicity interact to shape attitudes about running for political office (Silva and Skulley 2019; Holman and Schneider 2018; Shames 2015). Future research might examine whether the race and ethnicity of a role model interacts with gender and portrayed career goals to shape interest in a political career (Schneider and Bos 2019). As the composition of Congress changes, such questions become even more crucial to answer.

A key consideration is the use of a lay population rather than a pool of "likely candidates" used in other research (Lawless and Fox 2010).

Crowder-Meyer's (2018) recent work on political ambition in the general population underscores the importance of understanding the difference between factors of significance in the general population or from an elite sample. Our work underscores the importance of considering context and sample in studies of political ambition.

Candidate-training organizations, leadership training for college students, and classroom interventions are now common methods for increasing women's political ambition and improving the number of women running for office (Kreitzer and Osborn 2018). Introducing speakers who act as role models is often a strategy of these programs, yet there have been few systematic studies of the effects. Using the results from a survey conducted before and after one campaign training, Sweet-Cushman and Schneider (Schneider and Sweet-Cushman forthcoming; Sweet-Cushman 2018) found that attendees were likely to identify a role model from the training as influential and inspired feelings of closeness, though, as with our findings here, there were no significant effects of the training on political ambition. Interestingly, the training affected how the women viewed a political career; after the training, as compared to before, the women were far more likely to say that the political career afforded the opportunity to pursue power-related goals (Schneider and Sweet-Cushman forthcoming). These findings further underscore the need for more work on the power and limitations of role models to change women's relationship to a political career.

Our colleagues investigating how to improve women's presence in STEM careers have made greater strides on producing research that can be used in shaping policy changes (Diekman et al. 2017). We expect that social scientists interested in achieving parity for women in the political realm will soon follow their example.

Note

1. We chose not to include men because frames and other manipulations often do not affect men (Schneider et al. 2016; Preece and Stoddard 2015a).

References

Alexander, Amy C. 2012. "Change in Women's Descriptive Representation and the Belief in Women's Ability to Govern: A Virtuous Cycle." *Politics & Gender* 8 (4): 437–64.

Associated Press. April 9, 2019. "Sen. Gillibrand Calls Hillary Clinton 'a Role Model for All.'" By Juana Summers.

Atkeson, Lonna Rae. 2003. "Not All Cues Are Created Equal: The Conditional Impact of Female Candidates on Political Engagement." *Journal of Politics* 65 (4): 1040–61.

Bakan, David. 1966. *The Duality of Human Existence: Isolation and Communion in Western Man.* Boston: Beacon Press. catalog.hathitrust.org/api/volumes/oclc /2008471.html.

Barnes, Tiffany D., and Mirya R. Holman. Forthcoming. "Gender Quotas, Women's Representation, and Legislative Diversity." *Journal of Politics.*

———. 2018. "Taking Diverse Backgrounds into Account in Studies of Political Ambition and Representation." *Politics, Groups, and Identities,* November, 1–13.

Beauregard, Katrine. 2017. "Quotas and Gender Gaps in Political Participation among Established Industrial European Democracies: Distinguishing Within- and Across-Country Effects." *Political Research Quarterly* 70 (3): 657–72.

Berinsky, Adam J., Gregory A. Huber, and Gabriel Lenz. 2012. "Evaluating Online Labor Markets for Experimental Research: Amazon.com's Mechanical Turk." *Political Analysis* 20 (3).

Betz, Diana E., and Denise Sekaquaptewa. 2012. "My Fair Physicist? Feminine Math and Science Role Models Demotivate Young Girls." *Social Psychological and Personality Science* 3 (6): 738–46.

Bonneau, Chris W., and Kristin Kanthak. 2018. "Stronger Together: Political Ambition and the Presentation of Women Running for Office." *Politics, Groups, and Identities,* November, 1–19.

Broockman, David E. 2014. "Do Female Politicians Empower Women to Vote or Run for Office? A Regression Discontinuity Approach." *Electoral Studies* 34 (June): 190–204.

Brown, Nadia E. 2014a. *Sisters in the Statehouse: Black Women and Legislative Decision Making.* Oxford, UK: Oxford University Press.

———. 2014b. "Political Participation of Women of Color: An Intersectional Analysis." *Journal of Women, Politics & Policy* 35 (4): 315–48.

Buunk, Abraham P., José Maria Peiró, and Chris Griffioen. 2007. "A Positive Role Model May Stimulate Career-Oriented Behavior." *Journal of Applied Social Psychology* 37 (7): 1489–1500.

Campbell, David E., and Christina Wolbrecht. 2006. "See Jane Run: Women Politicians as Role Models for Adolescents." *Journal of Politics* 68 (2): 233–47.

———. 2019. "The Resistance as Role Model: Disillusionment and Protest among American Adolescents after 2016." *Political Behavior,* February.

Cargile, Ivy. 2016. "Latina Issues: An Analysis of the Policy Issue Competencies of Latina Candidates." In *Distinct Identities: Minority Women in U.S. Politics,* ed. Nadia E. Brown and Sarah Allen Gershon. New York: Routledge, Taylor & Francis Group.

Carroll, Susan J., and Kira Sanbonmatsu. 2013. *More Women Can Run: Gender and Pathways to the State Legislatures.* Oxford, UK: Oxford University Press.

Center for American Women and Politics. 2019. "Current Numbers." www.cawp .rutgers.edu/current-numbers.

Cheryan, Sapna, Benjamin J. Drury, and Marissa Vichayapai. 2013. "Enduring Influence of Stereotypical Computer Science Role Models on Women's Academic Aspirations." *Psychology of Women Quarterly* 37 (1): 72–79.

Cheryan, Sapna, John Oliver Siy, Marissa Vichayapai, Benjamin J. Drury, and Saenam Kim. 2011. "Do Female and Male Role Models Who Embody STEM Stereotypes Hinder Women's Anticipated Success in STEM?" *Social Psychological and Personality Science* 2 (6): 656–64.

Clark, Emily K., Melissa A. Fuesting, and Amanda B. Diekman. 2016. "Enhancing Interest in Science: Exemplars as Cues to Communal Affordances of Science." *Journal of Applied Social Psychology* 46 (11): 641–54.

Clayton, Amanda. 2015. "Women's Political Engagement under Quota-Mandated Female Representation: Evidence from a Randomized Policy Experiment." *Comparative Political Studies* 48 (3): 333–69.

Congressional Management Foundation and Society for Human Resource Management. 2013. "Life in Congress: The Member Perspective." Washington, DC.

Crowder-Meyer, Melody. 2018. "Baker, Bus Driver, Babysitter, Candidate? Revealing the Gendered Development of Political Ambition among Ordinary Americans." *Political Behavior,* September.

Dasgupta, Nilanjana. 2011. "Ingroup Experts and Peers as Social Vaccines Who Inoculate the Self-Concept: The Stereotype Inoculation Model." *Psychological Inquiry* 22 (4): 231–46.

Diekman, Amanda B., and Monica C. Schneider. 2010. "A Social Role Theory Perspective on Gender Gaps in Political Attitudes." *Psychology of Women Quarterly* 34 (4): 486–97.

Diekman, Amanda B., Emily K. Clark, Amanda M. Johnston, Elizabeth R. Brown, and Mia Steinberg. 2011. "Malleability in Communal Goals and Beliefs Influences Attraction to STEM Careers: Evidence for a Goal Congruity Perspective." *Journal of Personality and Social Psychology* 101 (5): 902–18.

Diekman, Amanda B., Mia Steinberg, Elizabeth R. Brown, Aimee L. Belanger, and Emily K. Clark. 2017. "A Goal Congruity Model of Role Entry, Engagement, and Exit: Understanding Communal Goal Processes in STEM Gender Gaps." *Personality and Social Psychology Review* 21 (2): 142–75.

Dittmar, Kelly, Kira Sanbonmatsu, and Susan J. Carroll. 2018. *A Seat at the Table: Congresswomen's Perspectives on Why Their Presence Matters.* New York: Oxford University Press.

Elder, Laurel. 2004. "Why Women Don't Run: Explaining Women's Underrepresentation in America's Political Institutions." *Women & Politics* 26 (2): 27–56.

Farris, Emily M., and Mirya R. Holman. 2014. "Social Capital and Solving the Puzzle of Black Women's Political Participation." *Politics, Groups, and Identities* 2 (3): 331–49.

Fuesting, Melissa A., and Amanda B. Diekman. 2017. "Not by Success Alone: Role Models Provide Pathways to Communal Opportunities in STEM." *Personality and Social Psychology Bulletin* 43 (2): 163–76.

Gilardi, Fabrizio. 2015. "The Temporary Importance of Role Models for Women's Political Representation." *American Journal of Political Science* 59 (4): 957–70.

Greenlee, Jill S., Mirya R. Holman, and Rachel VanSickle-Ward. 2014. "Making It Personal: Assessing the Impact of In-Class Exercises on Closing the Gender Gap in Political Ambition." *Journal of Political Science Education* 10 (1): 48–61.

Herrmann, Sarah D., Robert Mark Adelman, Jessica E. Bodford, Oliver Graudejus, Morris A. Okun, and Virginia S. Y. Kwan. 2016. "The Effects of a Female Role Model on Academic Performance and Persistence of Women in STEM Courses." *Basic and Applied Social Psychology* 38 (5): 258–68.

Holman, Mirya R., and Monica C. Schneider. 2018. "Gender, Race, and Political Ambition: How Intersectionality and Frames Influence Interest in Political Office." *Politics, Groups, and Identities* 6 (2): 264–80.

Hoyt, Crystal L. 2013. "Inspirational or Self-Deflating: The Role of Self-Efficacy in Elite Role Model Effectiveness." *Social Psychological and Personality Science* 4 (3): 290–98.

Hoyt, Crystal L., Jeni L. Burnette, and Audrey N. Innella. 2012. "I Can Do That: The Impact of Implicit Theories on Leadership Role Model Effectiveness." *Personality and Social Psychology Bulletin* 38 (2): 257–68.

Hoyt, Crystal L., and Stefanie Simon. 2011. "Female Leaders: Injurious or Inspiring Role Models for Women?" *Psychology of Women Quarterly* 35 (1): 143–57.

Jordan, Mary. November 8, 2018. "Record Number of Women Heading to Congress." *Washington Post*. www.washingtonpost.com/politics/record-number-of-women-appear-headed-for-congress/2018/11/06/76a9e60a-e1eb-11e8-8f5f-a55347f48762_story.html?utm_term=.21d0400a721b.

Kanthak, Kristin, and Jonathan Woon. 2015. "Women Don't Run? Election Aversion and Candidate Entry." *American Journal of Political Science* 59 (3): 595–612.

Karp, Jeffrey A., and Susan A. Banducci. 2008. "When Politics Is Not Just a Man's Game: Women's Representation and Political Engagement." *Electoral Studies* 27 (1): 105–15.

Kreitzer, Rebecca J., and Tracy L. Osborn. 2018. "The Emergence and Activities of Women's Recruiting Groups in the U.S." *Politics, Groups, and Identities*, November, 1–11.

Krupnikov, Yanna, and Adam Seth Levine. 2014. "Cross-Sample Comparisons and External Validity." *Journal of Experimental Political Science* 1 (1): 59–80.

Ladam, Christina, Jeffrey J. Harden, and Jason H. Windett. 2018. "Prominent Role Models: High-Profile Female Politicians and the Emergence of Women as Candidates for Public Office." *American Journal of Political Science* 62 (2): 369–81.

Landau, Mark J., Daphna Oyserman, Lucas A. Keefer, and George C. Smith. 2014. "The College Journey and Academic Engagement: How Metaphor Use Enhances Identity-Based Motivation." *Journal of Personality and Social Psychology* 106 (5): 679–98.

Lawless, Jennifer L., and Richard L. Fox. 2010. *It Still Takes a Candidate: Why Women Don't Run for Office.* New York: Cambridge University Press.

Lawson, Katie M., and Hilary M. Lips. 2014. "The Role of Self-Perceived Agency and Job Attainability in Women's Impressions of Successful Women in Masculine Occupations: Agency and Impressions of Successful Women." *Journal of Applied Social Psychology* 44 (6): 433–41.

Lent, Robert W., Steven D. Brown, and Gail Hackett. 2002. "Social Cognitive Career Theory." In *Career Choice and Development,* ed. Duane Brown, 4th ed., 255–311. San Francisco: Jossey-Bass.

Lizotte, Mary-Kate. 2020. "Women's and Men's Identities and 2018 Vote Choice." In *Politicking While Female: The Political Lives of Women,* ed. Nichole M. Bauer. Baton Rouge: Louisiana State University Press.

Lockwood, Penelope. 2006. "'Someone Like Me Can Be Successful': Do College Students Need Same-Gender Role Models?" *Psychology of Women Quarterly* 30 (1): 36–46.

Lockwood, Penelope, and Ziva Kunda. 1997. "Superstars and Me: Predicting the Impact of Role Models on the Self." *Journal of Personality and Social Psychology* 73 (1): 91–103.

Mansbridge, Jane. 1999. "Should Blacks Represent Blacks and Women Represent Women? A Contingent 'Yes.'" *Journal of Politics* 61 (3): 628–57.

Mariani, Mack, Bryan W. Marshall, and A. Lanethea Mathews-Schultz. 2015. "See Hillary Clinton, Nancy Pelosi, and Sarah Palin Run? Party, Ideology, and the Influence of Female Role Models on Young Women." *Political Research Quarterly* 68 (4): 716–31.

McCall, Leslie. 2005. "The Complexity of Intersectionality." *Signs: Journal of Women in Culture and Society* 30 (3): 1771–1800.

O'Brien, Laurie T., Aline Hitti, Emily Shaffer, Amanda R. Van Camp, Donata Henry, and Patricia N. Gilbert. 2017. "Improving Girls' Sense of Fit in Science: Increasing the Impact of Role Models." *Social Psychological and Personality Science* 8 (3): 301–9.

Pitkin, Hanna F. 1967. *The Concept of Representation*. Berkeley: University of California Press.

Pomaki, Georgia, Paul Karoly, and Stan Maes. 2009. "Linking Goal Progress to Subjective Well-Being at Work: The Moderating Role of Goal-Related Self-Efficacy and Attainability." *Journal of Occupational Health Psychology* 14 (2): 206–18.

Preece, Jessica Robinson, and Olga Stoddard. 2015a. "Why Women Don't Run: Experimental Evidence on Gender Differences in Political Competition Aversion." *Journal of Economic Behavior & Organization* 117 (September): 296–308.

———. 2015b. "Does the Message Matter? A Field Experiment on Political Party Recruitment." *Journal of Experimental Political Science* 2 (1): 26–35.

Richards, Zoe, and Miles Hewstone. 2001. "Subtyping and Subgrouping: Processes for the Prevention and Promotion of Stereotype Change." *Personality and Social Psychology Review* 5 (1): 52–73.

Rickabaugh, Cheryl A. 1995. "College Students' Stereotypes of Gender and Political Activism." *Basic and Applied Social Psychology* 16 (3): 319–31.

Schneider, Monica C., and Angela L. Bos. 2019. "The Application of Social Role Theory to the Study of Gender in Politics." *Political Psychology* 40 (S1): 173–213.

Schneider, Monica C., and Jennie Sweet-Cushman. 2020. "Pieces of Women's Political Ambition Puzzle: Changing Perceptions of a Political Career with Campaign Training." In *Good Reasons to Run,* ed. Shauna L. Shames, Rachel Bernhard, Mirya R. Holman, and Dawn Teele. Philadelphia: Temple University Press.

Schneider, Monica C., Mirya R. Holman, Amanda B. Diekman, and Thomas McAndrew. 2016. "Power, Conflict, and Community: How Gendered Views of Political Power Influence Women's Political Ambition: Power, Conflict, and Community." *Political Psychology* 37 (4): 515–31.

Shames, Shauna L. 2015. "American Women of Color and Rational Non-Candidacy: When Silent Citizenship Makes Politics Look like Old White Men Shouting." *Citizenship Studies* 19 (5): 553–69.

———. 2017. *Out of the Running: Why Millennials Reject Political Careers and Why It Matters*. New York: New York University Press.

Silva, Andrea, and Carrie Skulley. 2019. "Always Running: Candidate Emergence among Women of Color over Time." *Political Research Quarterly* 72 (2): 342–59.

Stout, Jane G., Nilanjana Dasgupta, Matthew Hunsinger, and Melissa A. McManus. 2011. "STEMing the Tide: Using Ingroup Experts to Inoculate Women's Self-Concept in Science, Technology, Engineering, and Mathematics (STEM)." *Journal of Personality and Social Psychology* 100 (2): 255–70.

Sweet-Cushman, Jennie. 2016. "Gender, Risk Assessment, and Political Ambition." *Politics and the Life Sciences* 35 (2): 1–17.

———. 2018. "See It; Be It? The Use of Role Models in Campaign Trainings for Women." *Politics, Groups, and Identities,* November, 1–11.

Wolak, Jenny. 2015. "Candidate Gender and the Political Engagement of Women and Men." *American Politics Research* 45 (3): 827–96.

Wolbrecht, Christina, and David E. Campbell. 2007. "Leading by Example: Female Members of Parliament as Political Role Models." *American Journal of Political Science* 51 (4): 921–39.

———. 2017. "Role Models Revisited: Youth, Novelty, and the Impact of Female Candidates." *Politics, Groups, and Identities* 5 (3): 418–34.

Yglesias, Matthew. November 7, 2016. "A Hillary Clinton Presidency Will Greatly Boost Women's Representation in Politics, with Big Policy Consequences." *Vox.* www.vox.com/2016/6/6/11829852/clinton-woman-effect.

Zetterberg, Pär. 2009. "Do Gender Quotas Foster Women's Political Engagement? Lessons from Latin America." *Political Research Quarterly* 62 (4): 715–30.

GENDER ON
THE CAMPAIGN TRAIL

VOTING FOR MULTIRACIAL WOMEN

DANIELLE CASAREZ LEMI

Recent developments in American politics have led to a resurgent need to consider diversity among women as voters, particularly the differences in how white women and women of color voters behave politically (Junn 2017; Frasure-Yokley 2018). In 2018, numerous women of color ran for office, including high-profile figures such as Alexandria Ocasio-Cortez and Ilhan Omar. In the summer of 2019, another high-profile woman of color sought the presidential nomination: US Senator Kamala Harris. Harris is one of three women of color as well as one of the three biracial women in the Senate, as Harris is black and Asian American. Like Harris, Tammy Duckworth and Catherine Cortez Masto have biracial backgrounds.

While Harris would have been the first black and Asian American woman to become president of the United States, she also would have been the first biracial woman to claim the title. Harris's run for office reflects broader demographic changes in the United States. The two-or-more-races population in the country is among the fastest growing, and it has inspired a literature on the implications of multiracial identification for political attitudes (Masuoka 2017; Davenport 2018). Multiracial identification is also more common among women than men (Davenport 2016). To date, however, we know very little about how voters respond to candidates with multiracial backgrounds, and I am not aware of any study to date that considers how female voters treat multiracial female candidates. I present findings from a survey experiment that manipulated whether a candidate was monoracial or multiracial. Generally, identifying a candidate as multiracial has no meaningful effect on most female voters. However, female voters with a sense of racial political consciousness are less likely to select multiracial female candidates from their own racial groups, and this is particularly true for Asian American women. These findings have implications for how we think about women's voting behavior and Kamala Harris's 2020 presidential run.

Race, Gender, and Descriptive Representation

Research on voter evaluations of candidates who share attributes with voters guides my expectations for how voters will respond to multiracial female candidates. The notion of *descriptive representation* is the idea that candidates and elected officials from marginalized groups enjoy a special relationship with their constituents (Pitkin 1967; Mansbridge 1999). Three strands of research have studied at length the extent to which voters from marginalized groups support candidates from their own groups in terms of race, sex, or race *and* sex.

A sense of linked fate, or racial political consciousness (Dawson 1994; Sanchez and Vargas 2016), has been found to be associated with preferences for same-race representatives (Schildkraut 2013, 2017). The idea is that, by supporting candidates with whom they share a race, voters with a sense of linked fate are making a rational decision (Dawson 1994; Sanchez and Masuoka 2010), as nonwhite descriptive representatives are those most likely to advocate for marginalized nonwhite communities (Minta and Sinclair-Chapman 2013; Minta and Brown 2014). Although the concept of linked fate was developed from black American politics, it has been used to understand the political behaviors of multiple racial groups (Sanchez and Vargas 2016; Gay, Hochschild, and White 2016). When it comes to evaluations of political candidates, research to date suggests that those with racial linked fate are those more likely to select candidates from their own racial group (McConnaughy et al. 2010; Schildkraut 2013, 2017).

In a similar vein, other research has examined whether women support female candidates. The evidence to date suggests women's support for female candidates may vary by policy preferences, partisanship, and race. For instance, using data from the National Election Study, Dolan (2008) tested the "gender affinity effect," or the idea that women will support women, and found that women express greater favorability toward Democratic female candidates, but not Republican female candidates. In Brians

(2005), longitudinal data from the National Election Study suggests that, while Republicans may be willing to support Democratic women over Republican men, ultimately, female voters support female candidates from their own party. In an experiment, Martin (2019) showed that women's support for female candidates may also depend on the candidate's own ideology and issue positions. A recent study by Merolla, Sellers, and Lemi (2017) using two experiments confirmed that women are not more likely to select a female candidate than a male candidate—issue positions and partisan affiliation are more important to women than a candidate's sex. In short, while voters may have same-race preferences, research to date does not suggest female voters have strong same-gender preferences.

The two preceding sets of research focus on whether candidates' race *or* their sex pushes voters from those racial and gender groups to vote for them. By contrast, studies on candidate evaluation from an intersectional perspective consider how race *and* sex interact to produce outcomes (Hancock 2007). The findings from this body of work may be counterintuitive to some: women of color enjoy electoral advantages (Bejarano 2013; Philpot and Walton 2007). For example, Bejarano (2013) argues that Latinas, because of "gender expectations" associated with being a woman, can appeal to voters who might otherwise hesitate to vote for a Latino. Philpot and Walton (2007) found that, in a hypothetical match-up between a black female candidate and a white male candidate, the black female candidate collected majorities of black women, black men, white women, and white men voters. Analytical approaches that take race *and* sex into account suggest we should not be that surprised when women do not uniformly support female candidates—women's responses to female candidates may depend on their own race (Junn 2017) and their own racial position in the American racial hierarchy (Masuoka and Junn 2013). For instance, white women in particular do not express strong preferences for white female descriptive representation (Phillips 2018; Cassese and Barnes forthcoming). Philpot and Walton (2007) suggest that support for black women among black women may be a function of black women's sense of linked fate with other black women.

While previous research underscores how voters respond to candidates who share their race, sex, or race *and* sex, current events raise questions about the viability of *multiracial* candidates, or candidates identified with at least two racial categories. Does being a multiracial female candidate even matter for vote choice? Do multiracial female candidates hold an advantage over monoracial female candidates? Little is known about voters' responses to multiracial female candidates, and what exists is limited to multiracial male elected officials. One experiment about Charles Rangel, who is black and Puerto Rican, found that, when Rangel was framed as Latino, Latinos were not as forthcoming in their positive evaluations of Rangel as African American participants were (Adida, Davenport, and McClendon 2016). In another study about a black and white candidate who varied in his claimed identity, college students viewed him as weaker on civil rights competency when he identified as "biracial," relative to when he identified as black (Masuoka 2015). What is left is research about Barack Obama, whose presidency was marked by racial resentment from whites (Piston 2010, Tesler 2016). Ultimately, the literature is not clear on how multiracial *female* candidates may be received.

Theory and Hypotheses

I draw on a social identity framework to examine how female voters will respond to female multiracial candidates. Multiracial female candidates, because they have the combination of being female and being assigned to two racial categories, may incur an advantage over monoracial female candidates when competing for votes from women outside their own racial group, but a disadvantage when competing for votes from women within their own group.

The social identity theory of leadership posits the idea that group leaders represent group prototypes (Hogg and Reid 2006; Hogg 2001), or the "ideal" version of the group member. Those who fit group prototypes are those who are likely to cultivate support from the group to become a group leader (Hogg 2001). For example, consider the case of Latinos and the rhetoric surrounding Latino candidates who do not speak Spanish, like Ted Cruz (Lavariega Monforti et al. 2013). Candidates who do not fit neatly into group prototypes, like multiracial candidates who belong to multiple racial categories, are unlikely to be viewed as preferable to a monoracial candidate. If a candidate is identified with multiple categories, his or her mere identification with more than one racial group may raise confusion about exactly how the candidate personally identifies and with whom he or she aligns racially—especially among those with stronger racial identities who may feel inclined to enforce group boundaries (Dalmage 2000).

Research on multiracial people suggests that some multiracial persons experience questions of authenticity (Romo 2011). For instance, Kamala Harris has faced questions about whether she is "black enough" due to her Jamaican heritage, and implicitly, her multiracial background (Vagianos 2019). By contrast, three years ago, Tammy Duckworth, who is white and Asian, was mocked by a political opponent who discounted her white father's longstanding connection to the United States, depicting both her parents as Thai immigrants (Diaz and Scott 2016). A common experience for multiracial people is that outsiders often have trouble "reading" their racial backgrounds (Remedios and Chasteen 2013). Thus it is possible that, when appealing to female voters, multiracial female candidates will be less likely to receive the support of female voters from their own racial group. By virtue of their classification in two racial categories, female voters may receive a signal that the candidate is unlike the rest of the racial group (Fenno 1978). In turn, the use of race as a heuristic (Dawson 1994; Sanchez and Masuoka 2010; McConnaughy et al. 2010) becomes more difficult, as voters cannot make quick inferences about the multiracial candidate because her multiracial classification makes her non-prototypical (Hogg 2001).

On the other hand, multiracial female candidates may incur an advantage when appealing to female voters from outside their racial group. This argument stems from the idea that individuals who have membership to multiple categories experience group stereotypes differently (Purdie-Vaughns and Eibach 2008). Indeed, this idea is demonstrated by scholarship on female candidates of color, whose sex "softens" their race because of feminine stereotypes (Bejarano 2013). Multiracial women are often viewed as "exotic" (Hall 2004) and commonly asked, "What are you?" (Hall 2004). Because multiracial identification is not in line with dominant understandings of racial categories (Omi and Winant 1994), multiracial identification may disrupt the efficiency of race as a heuristic to select a candidate (Dawson 1994; McConnaughy et al. 2010; Schildkraut 2013, 2017). This study thus aims to examine how female voters respond to female candidates who vary in race and discerns whether female voters draw distinctions between monoracial and multiracial female candidates. From this discussion flows three hypotheses:

(H1) Relative to a monoracial in-group female candidate, monoracial female voters will be less likely to select an in-group multiracial female candidate. If this is true, multiracial female candidates who share a race with the respondent will have a negative effect on vote choice, relative to a monoracial candidate who shares a race with the respondent.

(H2) Relative to a monoracial out-group female candidate, monoracial female voters will be more likely to select in-group *and* out-group multiracial female candidates. If this is true, multiracial female candidates will have a positive effect on vote choice, relative to monoracial candidates who do not share a race with the respondent.

(H3) Support for multiracial female candidates will depend on racial linked fate, such that the effect of multiracial identification interacts with a female voter's sense of racial linked fate. If this is true, we should see a statistically significant interaction between an individual's reported racial linked fate and exposure to a multiracial female candidate.

Data and Method

These hypotheses were tested using data from a conjoint survey experiment fielded in May 2016. This design comes from marketing techniques (Orme 2010; Hainmueller, Hopkins, and Yamamoto 2014), and is similar to consumer surveys in which companies solicit preferences for products that may vary in price, color, or size, for instance. In this design, market researchers are trying to figure out what consumers value most in a product—is it price? Is it size and portability? Is it color and aesthetics? For this study, the design is most useful for giving voters a lot of information about a candidate to see if race still pushes them toward specific candidates.

The survey was conducted online using Qualtrics survey panels. To ensure an adequate sample size to analyze the behavior of each racial group, at least 200 participants per racial group were sampled (Orme 2010). The sample is entirely people who identified with one racial category. This sample consisted of 93 white women, 100 black women, 101 Asian women, and 92 Hispanic women. About 55% of this sample identified as Democrats and about 17% as Republicans. About 22% considered themselves independents, and about 7% did not identify as Democrat, Republican, or independent. The average age of this sample was thirty-four years.

In this conjoint experiment design, participants entered a survey and answered a series of demographic and attitudinal questions and then saw ten pairs of candidate profiles that randomly varied in race (Asian, black, Hispanic, white, Asian and white, Asian and black, Asian and Hispanic, black and white, black and Asian, black and Hispanic, Hispanic and white), gender (male, female), nativity (born in the United States, born outside the United States), partisan affiliation (Democrat, Republican, independent), ideology (liberal, moderate, conservative), and political experience (served in city council, served in the state legislature, served in Congress). They were told to imagine these candidates were running for Congress. As they saw each pair, they were asked to select the candidate they would support. For each individual respondent, there are twenty observations, as they were presented with two candidates ten times. Here I am interested in one outcome: On average, was the respondent more likely to vote for a female candidate, given they had a multiracial background relative to a monoracial one? Linear regression with clustered standard errors by respondent was used to assess the hypotheses (Hainmueller, Hopkins, and Yamamoto 2014).

Findings

I report the findings in table 3.1 below. Table 3.1 reports the average change in probability that a female candidate with a given attribute was selected, relative to a reference-category attribute, with clustered standard errors (Hainmueller, Hopkins, and Yamamoto 2014). For example, the reference category for race is "monoracial." "Multiracial" is the category to which "monoracial" is being compared. The estimate indicates the *average change* of the probability of being selected relative to the reference category, *not* the probability of being selected. The estimates indicate the difference from the baseline categories. Contrary to what previous research suggests, in this study, multiracial categorization does not matter much to women voters selecting between female candidates. I do not find support for H1 in table 3.1. Women are more likely to prefer monoracial candidates with whom they share a race by about 15% (p = 0.000), and out-group multiracial candidates do not reach statistical significance (0.0149, p = 0.449).

Table 3.1 Average Change in Probability of Selecting a Multiracial Female Candidate Relative to a Monoracial Female Candidate

Multiracial	0.0149	(0.0197)
R's Race	0.148***	(0.0287)
Multiracial # R's Race	−0.0568*	(0.0344)
Born outside the US	−0.127***	(0.0177)
Republican	−0.0791**	(0.0239)
Independent	0.0408*	(0.0214)
Moderate	−0.00529	(0.0214)
Conservative	−0.0996***	(0.0238)
Served in City Council	−0.0684***	(0.0194)
Served in State Legislature	−0.00105	(0.0186)
R's Party	0.150***	(0.0204)
Constant	0.565***	(0.0280)
Observations	3868	
R^2	0.0723	

* $p < 0.10$
** $p < 0.05$
*** $p < 0.001$.

Note: Standard errors in parentheses.

Additionally, there is a negative interaction between multiracial candidates and sharing a race with the candidate that reaches marginal statistical significance and lends support to H2 (−0.06, $p = 0.100$).

Furthermore, women clearly prefer Democratic women relative to Republican female candidates, as Republican females are penalized by about 8% ($p = 0.001$). This partisan preference exists when accounting for shared partisanship with the candidates (Merolla, Sellers, and Lemi 2017). Rather than selecting candidates based on their race as multiracial or monoracial, women in this sample prefer female candidates who were born in the United States, are Democrats, liberal, and who have congressional experience. Indeed, women are significantly more likely to vote for female candidates who share their partisan identification by about 15% ($p = 0.000$). These findings are in line with what others have found about the importance of partisanship and female voters (Dolan 2008; Merolla, Sellers, and Lemi 2017). While there is a general preference for monoracial in-group candidates relative to monoracial out-group candidates, female voters do not differentiate between in-group monoracial and in-group multiracial female candidates. Instead, female voters place the most weight on shared partisanship with the candidate.

While the first analysis considers women as a whole, it does not take into account structural differences in political socialization for women in each racial group (Masuoka and Junn 2013; Junn 2017; Brown 2014). For instance, perhaps the effect of multiracial identification looks different among white women than it does for black, Asian, or Hispanic women. Figure 3.1 disaggregates the results in table 3.1 by race of female voter and whether the candidates were from the voter's racial group. For simplicity, only the race coefficients are displayed in figure 3.1, but these estimates are from the full regression model that contains the rest of the candidate attributes. The bars are 95% confidence intervals, and bars that do not cross zero are statistically significant ($p > 0.05$).

As the left column shows, female voters of color are statistically significantly more likely to prefer an in-group monoracial candidate *and* in-group multiracial candidate. Relative to an in-group multiracial candidate, there is no statistically significant effect of being a multiracial out-group candidate on vote choice among any female voters. Thus, there is partial support for H1. Relative to out-group monoracial candidates, female voters of color are more likely to select multiracial in-group candidates. There is no statistically significant difference in being a multiracial female candidate relative to an outsider among female voters.

On the right side, the reference candidate is a monoracial in-group candidate. As the column shows, there is no statistically significant effect of being a multiracial in-group candidate, but the estimates trend negative across racial groups of female voters. Thus, there is no strong support for H2. These findings suggest that, for female voters evaluating female candidates, multiracial identification of a female candidate does not do much for female voters' choices.

There are also differences among racial groups (not shown). For ex-

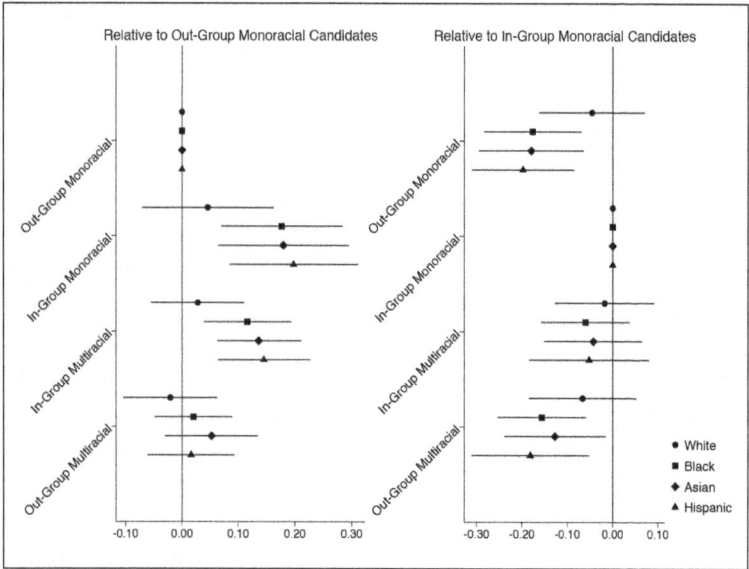

Figure 3.1. Average Change in Probability of Selection of a Multiracial Female Candidate Relative to In-Group and Out-Group Monoracial Female Candidates

Note: 95% confidence intervals included.

ample, nativity is the most important attribute determining white women's preferences, where white women are about 19% less likely to select a female candidate born outside the United States (p = 0.001). By contrast, for black women, the change in probability of selection is about 17% (p = 0.001). Additionally, for black women, nativity was not the most important attribute—whether a candidate was an in-group monoracial carried the most weight, increasing the probability of selection by about 18% (p = 0.001). For Hispanic women, the effect of being born in the United States drops to a change of just 9% (p = 0.026). Similar to black women, however, whether a candidate is an in-group monoracial is the most important attribute for Hispanic women (0.20, p = 0.001). For Asian women, the effect of nativity status on the selection of a candidate only reaches marginal statistical significance (−0.07, p = 0.059). Like black and Hispanic women, whether a candidate is an in-group monoracial is the most important attribute (0.1797, p = 0.003). That nativity is most important for white women is consistent with theories of racial hierarchy in the United

DANIELLE CASAREZ LEMI

States, where citizenship has historically been synonymous with whiteness (Masuoka and Junn 2013).

Similarly, shared partisanship was weighted differently among women. For white women, shared partisanship was the second-most important attribute in their vote choices; white women were about 16% more likely to select a female candidate that shared their partisanship ($p = 0.000$). Among Asian women, the effect of shared partisanship was an average change in about 18% ($0.176, p = 0.000$). For black women, shared partisanship only changed vote choice by about 12% ($p = 0.008$), and for Hispanic women, only about 9% ($p = 0.072$).

To determine whether racial linked fate interacts with multiracial identification (H3), I ran the same model, pooling all groups, and included an interaction term with whether female respondents felt a sense of linked fate with their racial group. Overall, female voters with a sense of racial linked fate are significantly less likely to select an in-group multiracial candidate by about 14% ($p = 0.019$). Additionally, they are also less likely to select an out-group monoracial by about 13% ($p = 0.032$), and an out-group multiracial candidate ($-0.11, p = 0.081$). This suggests that a sense of linked fate is a potential explanation for female voters' preferences for multiracial female candidates. These findings lend support to H3 and suggest that, on average, female voters with a sense of racial linked fate are more likely to penalize multiracial female candidates. These findings suggest that multiracial identification disrupts race as a political shortcut for multiracial female candidates courting female voters, even when information about multiracial female candidates' partisanship is included.

When I disaggregate by racial group, I find that racial linked fate moderates Asian women's choices for Asian female candidates. Asian women who felt a sense of linked fate were less likely to select a non-Asian female candidate about 22% ($p = 0.076$), and also less likely to select a multiracial Asian female candidate by about 25% ($p = 0.029$). For Asian women, linked fate moderates preferences for Asian female candidates, and Asian women with linked fate have a clear preference for monoracial Asian female candidates. There are three potential explanations for these findings. First, although research on Asian Americans indicates that fewer Asian Americans identify as "Asian American" than as a member of a specific group (Wong et al. 2011), it is possible that Asian American women in particular have a heightened sense of race-gender consciousness and preference for monoracial same-race candidates (Gershon et al. forthcoming). As a result, it is possible that Asian American women recognize monoracial female Asian candidates as the only suitable representatives capable of advancing Asian American issues. Second, Asian American women in this sample may have a more rigid idea of what constitutes the category "Asian" than other women in each racial group in this sample. Because of this, multiracial identification of an Asian female candidate may clash with this sample's idea of the "ideal Asian representative." Third, previous research has indicated that Asian American linked fate is malleable and may shift in response to exposure to descriptive representatives (Junn and Masuoka 2008). This malleability may explain why multiracial identification of an Asian female candidate disrupts race as a heuristic for Asian female voters. If pan-ethnic linked fate tends to be weak among Asian Americans generally, then exposure to a candidate who is only partially Asian may activate linked fate, but in a negative direction.

Discussion and Conclusion

I find some evidence that female voters are more likely to vote for multiracial female candidates relative to monoracial outsiders. The attributes that push women voters to select a given female candidate are nativity, partisanship, and political experience. For Asian American women, a sense of racial linked fate may pull Asian women voters *away* from multiracial Asian female candidates.

Taken together, these findings have three implications for theories of descriptive representation and intersectional analytical frameworks. First, when women must select among female candidates, on average, they are more likely to select a multiracial female candidate when the reference candidate is an outsider; there is no difference when the reference candidate is an insider. Women generally prefer female candidates who share their race. Second, female voters differentiate among female candidates. Women do not simply vote for any female candidate. Just because women share a sex attribute with female candidates does not negate the importance of other attributes, such as nativity and shared partisanship. Third, it is important to consider heterogeneous effects on subpopulations of categories (Lemi and Brown forthcoming; Hancock 2007; Masuoka and Junn 2013). While multiracial identification had a statistically significant effect on women of color relative to an out-group monoracial, this effect did not extend to white women. Multiracial identification may be more consequential for voters who are women of color. Finally, as the United States becomes more diverse and efforts continue toward increased representation of racial minorities, multiracial female candidates may face barriers among female voters with a sense of racial linked fate. Ultimately, these findings raise questions about the extent to which traditional theories of the relationship between constituents and descriptive representatives will hold up as the multiracial population grows. Female voters draw distinctions between monoracial and multiracial female candidates, and demonstrate that traditional definitions of descriptive representatives constituting a single demographic category must be complicated. Future research should consider these effects on larger sample sizes.

What do these findings mean for 2020? The most obvious question is how women voters would have responded to Kamala Harris, a Democratic US senator who ran for president. These findings suggest that, generally, Harris's biracial background may have been attractive to black women and Asian women. Based on these findings, however, Harris may have faced obstacles among Asian American women who have a sense of racial linked fate. While previous research suggests that exposure to a same-race descriptive representative increases linked fate among Asian Americans (Junn and Masuoka 2008), among Asian American women with linked fate, Harris's multiracial Asian background may fall flat. For candidates like Harris, then, appeals to shared partisanship may ultimately be more effective in securing votes from Asian American women.

References

Adida, Claire L., Lauren D. Davenport, and Gwyneth McClendon. 2016. "Ethnic Cueing across Minorities: A Survey Experiment on Candidate Evaluation in the United States." *Public Opinion Quarterly* 80 (4): 816–36.

Barreto, Matt A. 2010. *Ethnic Cues: The Role of Shared Ethnicity in Latino Political Participation.* Ann Arbor: University of Michigan Press.

Bejarano, Christina E. 2013. *The Latina Advantage: Gender, Race, and Political Success.* Austin: University of Texas Press.

Brians, Craig Leonard. 2005. "Women for Women? Gender and Party Bias in Voting for Female Candidates." *American Politics Research* 33 (3): 357–75.

Brown, Nadia E. 2014. "Political Participation of Women of Color: An Intersectional Analysis." *Journal of Women, Politics & Policy* 35 (4): 315–48.

Cassese, Erin C., and Tiffany D. Barnes. 2019. "Reconciling Sexism and Women's Support for Republican Candidates: A Look at Gender, Class, and Whiteness in the 2012 and 2016 Presidential Races." *Political Behavior* 41: 677–700.

Dalmage, Heather M. 2000. *Tripping on the Color Line: Black-White Multiracial Families in a Racially Divided World.* New Brunswick, NJ: Rutgers University Press.

Davenport, Lauren D. 2016. "The Role of Gender, Class, and Religion in Biracial Americans' Labeling Decisions." *American Sociological Review* 8 (1): 57–84.

———. 2018. *Politics beyond Black and White: Biracial Identity and Attitudes in America.* New York: Cambridge University Press.

Dawson, Michael C. 1995. *Behind the Mule: Race and Class in African-American Politics.* Princeton, NJ: Princeton University Press.

Diaz, Daniella, and Eugene Scott. 2016. "Mark Kirk Apologizes for Using Tammy Duckworth's Thai Heritage in Debate Jab." *CNN.* October 28.

Dolan, Kathleen. 2008. "Is There a 'Gender Affinity Effect' in American Politics? Information, Affect, and Candidate Sex in U.S. House Elections." *Political Research Quarterly* 61 (1): 79–89.

Fenno, Richard F., Jr. 1978. *Home Style: House Members in Their Districts.* New York: Pearson, Addison-Wesley Publishers, Inc.

Frasure-Yokley, Lorrie. 2018. "Choosing the Velvet Glove: Women Voters, Ambivalent Sexism, and Vote Choice in 2016." *Journal of Race, Ethnicity, and Politics* 3 (Special Issue 1: Race, Religion, Gender and the 2016 U.S. Presidential Election): 3–25.

Gay, Claudine, Jennifer Hochschild and Ariel White. 2016. "Americans' Belief in Linked Fate: Does the Measure Capture the Concept?" *Journal of Race, Ethnicity, and Politics* 1: 117–44.

Gershon, Sarah Allen, Celeste Montoya, Christina Bejarano, and Nadia Brown. 2019. "Intersectional Linked Fate and Political Representation." *Politics, Groups, and Identities* 7 (3): 642–53.

Hainmueller, Jens, Daniel J. Hopkins, and Teppei Yamamoto. 2014. "Causal Inference in Conjoint Analysis: Understanding Multidimensional Choices via Stated Preference Experiments." *Political Analysis* 22 (1): 1–30.

Hall, Christine C. Iijima. 2004. "Mixed-Race Women." *Women & Therapy* 27 (1–2): 237–46.

Hancock, Ange-Marie. 2007. "When Multiplication Doesn't Equal Quick Addition: Examining Intersectionality as a Research Paradigm." *Perspectives on Politics* 5 (1): 63–79.

Hogg, Michael A. 2001. "A Social Identity Theory of Leadership." *Personality and Social Psychology Review* 5 (3): 184–200.

Hogg, Michael A., and Scott A. Reid. 2006. "Social Identity, Self-Categorization, and Communication of Group Norms." *Communication Theory* 16 (1): 7–30.

Junn, Jane. 2017. "The Trump Majority: White Womanhood and the Making of Female Voters in the U.S." *Politics, Groups and Identities* 5 (2): 343–52.

Junn, Jane, and Natalie Masuoka. 2008. "Asian American Identity: Shared Racial Status and Political Context." *Perspectives on Politics* 6 (4): 729–40.

Lavariega Monforti, Jessica, Melissa Michelson, and Ana B. Franco. 2013. "¿Por Quién Votará? Experimental Evidence about Language, Ethnicity and Vote Choice (among Republicans)." *Politics, Groups, & Identities* 1 (4): 475–87.

Lemi, Danielle Casarez, and Nadia E. Brown. 2019. "Melanin and Curls: Evaluation of Black Women Candidates." *Journal of Race, Ethnicity, and Politics* 4 (2): 259–96.

Mansbridge, Jane. 1999. "Should Blacks Represent Blacks and Women Represent Women? A Contingent 'Yes.'" *Journal of Politics* 61 (3): 628–57.

Martin, Danielle Joesten. 2019. "Playing the Women's Card: How Women Respond to Female Candidates' Descriptive Versus Substantive Representation." *American Politics Research* 47 (3): 549–81.

Masuoka, Natalie. 2015. "Racial Identification in a Post Obama Era: Multiracialism, Identity Choice, and Candidate Evaluation." In *American Identity in the Age of Obama*, ed. Amilcar Antonio Barreto and Richard L. O'Bryant. New York: Routledge, 42–69.

———. 2017. *Multiracial Identity and Racial Politics in the United States*. New York: Oxford University Press.

Masuoka, Natalie, and Jane Junn. 2013. *The Politics of Belonging: Race, Public Opinion, and Immigration*. Chicago: University of Chicago Press.

McConnaughy, Corrine M., Ismail K. White, David L. Leal, and Jason P. Casellas. 2010. "A Latino on the Ballot: Explaining Coethnic Voting Among Latinos and the Response of White Americans." *Journal of Politics* 72 (4): 1199–1211.

Merolla, Jennifer L., Abbylin H. Sellers, and Danielle Casarez Lemi. 2017. "Does the Presence of Women on the Ballot Increase Female Empowerment?" American Political Science Association Annual Meeting. San Francisco, August 31–September 2.

Minta, Michael D., and Nadia E. Brown. 2014. "Intersecting Interests: Gender, Race, and Congressional Attention to Women's Issues." *Du Bois Review: Social Science Research on Race* 11 (2): 253–72.

Minta, Michael D., and Valeria Sinclair-Chapman. 2013. "Diversity in Political Institutions and Congressional Responsiveness to Minority Interests." *Political Research Quarterly* 68 (1): 127–40.

Omi, Michael, and Howard Winant. 1994. *Racial Formation in the United States from the 1960s to the 1990s*. 2nd ed. New York: Routledge.

Orme, Bryan K. 2010. *Getting Started with Conjoint Analysis: Strategies for Product Design and Pricing Research*. 2nd ed. Glendale, CA: Research Publishers LLC.

Phillips, Christian. 2018. "Wanting, and Weighting: White Women and Descriptive Representation in the 2016 Presidential Election." *Journal of Race, Ethnicity, and Politics* 3 (S1): 29–51.

Philpot, Tasha S., and Hanes Walton, Jr. 2007. "One of Our Own: Black Female Candidates and the Voters Who Support Them." *American Journal of Political Science* 51 (1): 49–62.

Piston, Spencer. 2010. "How Explicit Racial Prejudice Hurt Obama in the 2008 Election." *Political Behavior* 32 (4): 431–51.

Pitkin, Hannah. 1967. *The Concept of Representation.* Berkeley: University of California Press.

Purdie-Vaughns, Valerie, & Eibach, Richard P. 2008. "Intersectional Invisibility: The Distinctive Advantages and Disadvantages of Multiple Subordinate-Group Identities." *Sex Roles* 59(5/6), 377–91.

Remedios, Jessica D., and Alison L. Chasteen. 2013. "Finally, Someone Who 'Gets' Me! Multiracial People Value Others' Accuracy About Their Race." *Cultural Diversity and Ethnic Minority Psychology* 19 (4): 453–60.

Romo, Rebecca. 2011. "Between Black and Brown: Blaxican (Black-Mexican) Multiracial Identity in California." *Journal of Black Studies* 42: 402–26.

Sanchez, Gabriel R, and Eduardo Vargas. 2016. "Taking a Closer Look at Group Identity: The Link Between Theory and Measurement of Group Consciousness and Linked Fate." *Political Research Quarterly* 69 (1): 160–74.

Sanchez, Gabriel R., and Natalie Masuoka. 2010. "Brown-Utility Heuristic? The Presence of Contributing Factors of Latino Linked Fate." *Hispanic Journal of Behavioral Sciences* 32 (4): 519–31.

Schildkraut, Deborah J. 2013. "Which Birds of a Feather Flock Together? Assessing Attitudes About Descriptive Representation Among Latinos and Asian Americans." *American Politics Research* 41 (4): 699–729.

———. 2017. "White Attitudes About Descriptive Representation in the U.S.: The Roles of Identity, Discrimination, and Linked Fate." *Politics, Groups, and Identities* 5 (1): 84–106.

Tesler, Michael. 2016. *Post-Racial or Most-Racial: Race and Politics in the Obama Era.* Chicago: University of Chicago Press.

Vagianos, Alanna. 2019. "Kamala Harris Responds to People Who Don't Think She's 'Black Enough.'" *Huffington Post.* July 16, 2019. www.huffpost.com/entry/kamala-harris-responds birtherism_n_5d2dc4eae4b0a873f641bcef.

Wong, Janelle, S. Karthick Ramakrishnan, Taeku Lee, and Jane Junn. 2011. *Asian American Political Participation: Emerging Constituents and Their Political Identities.* New York: Russell Sage Foundation.

DANIELLE CASAREZ LEMI

ON THE MONEY

Assessing the Campaign-Finance Networks of Women Congressional Candidates

ROSALYN COOPERMAN

I want to play in primaries, and I want to play big in primaries.

—STATEMENT FROM REP. ELISE STEFANIK, National Republican Congressional Committee (NRCC) Candidate Recruitment Chair, November 30, 2018

If that's what Elise wants to do, then that's her call,
her right, but I think that's a mistake.

—REP. TOM EMMER (R-MN),
incoming NRCC chairman, quoted December 4, 2018

I will continue speaking out ab[ou]t the crisis level of GOP women in Congress & will try to lead and change that by supporting strong GOP women candidates through my leadership PAC. But **NEWSFLASH** I wasn't asking for permission.

—TWEET FROM REP. STEFANIK (R-NY), December 4, 2018

Heading into the 2018 midterm elections, the National Republican Congressional Committee (NRCC) candidate recruitment chair, Representative Elise Stefanik (NY-21) was firing on all cylinders in her efforts to convince Republican women to run for the US House. She had recruited over one hundred women to run, a figure that the NRCC identified as "three times more female Republican candidates this cycle than in past election cycles."[1] And yet when the newly elected representatives assembled in January 2019 to be sworn into the 116th Congress, only one Republican woman, Carol Miller (WV-3), joined the thirty-five new

Democratic women as incoming freshmen, while the returning ranks of Republican women shrank from twenty-three to thirteen (CAWP 2018). Reflecting on her party's losses, Stefanik signaled her intention to get involved earlier in contests, particularly those featuring Republican women, which drew a rebuke from the incoming NRCC chair, who was reluctant for the party to get involved in congressional primaries. And while Stefanik's bold intention to provide early assistance in future elections will be welcome news to Republican female candidates, it addresses only one of many challenges facing the underdeveloped state of the campaign-finance networks available to them. This essay identifies those challenges and assesses their impact on women's political candidacy to Congress. I examine the campaign-finance networks of women's political action committees (PACs) that raised money for female congressional candidates in the 2018 midterm elections. I identify the women's PACs that were most active on behalf of female candidates, how many women they endorsed, how much money they raised, and where they directed those funds.

EMILY's List, the main liberal women's PAC, is unrivaled in the amount of money it raises to elect female candidates and is highly strategic in where it directs funds. By comparison, the three conservative women's PACs I profile, the Susan B. Anthony List, Value in Electing Women (VIEW) PAC, and Winning for Women, *combined* raised significantly less money for endorsed candidates. And, in the case of the Susan B. Anthony List, which raised the most of the three conservative women's PACs, it directed a majority of its funds to aid male, not female, Republican candidates. I also examine the efforts of conservative women's PACs in 2018 to support Carol Miller (R-WV), the only freshman Republican woman elected to the incoming 116th Congress. Miller's case is instructive in that it provides a template for how conservative women's PACs should fund the campaigns of the female candidates they endorse. But as this level of support by conservative women's PACs is very uncommon, I conclude that the funding infrastructure available to Democratic female candidates is significantly more developed and amplifies the party gap in women's representation in Congress that will likely persist through future election cycles.

* * *

ROSALYN COOPERMAN

Previous Research on Women's PACs

Extant literature on congressional elections indicates that campaigns are candidate focused, with fundraising associated with the electoral viability of candidates (Biersack, Herrnson, and Wilcox 1994; Dittmar 2015; Jacobson 1981; Kim and LeVeck 2013). Fundraising is often identified as a particular concern of women considering an electoral bid and is echoed by women officeholders running for reelection (Carroll and Sanbonmatsu 2013; Dittmar, Sanbonmatsu, and Carroll 2018; Jenkins 2007; Lawless and Fox 2010) even as women often raise as much, if not more, than men running in similarly situated contests (Burrell 1994). Scholars have also focused on donors and the campaign-finance networks available to female candidates as one explanation for why Democratic female candidates and officeholders outnumber female Republicans (see also Bryner and Weber 2013; Crespin and Deitz 2010; Crowder-Meyer and Cooperman 2018; Kitchens and Swers 2016; Thomsen and Swers 2017; but see Hannagan, Pimlott, and Littvay 2010 for a mixed interpretation).

Crowder-Meyer and Cooperman (2018) find that donors who contribute to liberal women's PACs are predominantly women and are particularly likely to identify as women's representation policy demanders (WRPDs), that is, they give money to these PACs and the Democratic Party with the stated purpose of electing more female candidates. WRPDs exist in conservative women's PACs and the Republican Party but are much less visible because the party's culture is much less receptive to group-based demands. Accordingly, Cooperman and Crowder-Meyer (2018) find that liberal women's PACs are better situated to promote women's representation in the Democratic Party than conservative women's PACs are in the Republican Party; they have closer ties to the party as they regularly contribute funds to its congressional campaign committees and state parties, and are more successful at raising large sums of money by aggressively fundraising from an enormous membership base, the majority of whom are women. Given the central role of campaign finance to political candidacy, it is important to examine more closely the role played by women's PACs in providing financial support to those women who ran and also the context of the 2018 election that made female donors a significant source of those funds.

The 2018 midterm congressional elections saw an unprecedented number of Democratic and Republican women running for office. The Center for American Women in Politics (CAWP), which tracks women's political candidacy, identified more than 500 women who filed to run for Congress, the majority of whom—by more than a two-to-one margin— were Democrats.[2] And if Democratic female candidates were fired up to run for Congress, female donors were particularly motivated to contribute to their campaigns. The Center for Responsive Politics tracked campaign contributions to congressional candidates by female donors from 1990 to 2018. It found that the starting point for contributions was essentially even, if not slightly to the advantage of Republican women, in the cumulative sums (under $2 million each) that female donors contributed to Democratic and Republican female candidates. The parity in donor giving reflected the parity in the number of women running as Democrats and Republicans. And it is important to bear in mind that the default electoral match-up in congressional elections is male candidates running against one another. Accordingly, through 2016, female donors contributed more money overall to men than to female congressional candidates. Also, when looking at the flow of contributions over time, the center found that the number of female donors' contributions to Republican female candidates remained flat while contributions to Democratic female candidates ticked upward, a trend that also reflected the sustained party gap in the number of female Democratic and Republican candidates through the 1990s to the present (Haley and Evers-Hillstrom 2019).

In analyzing contributions for 2018, the Center for Responsive Politics found that female donors contributed over $19 million for Republican female House and Senate candidates and over $159 million for female Democratic congressional candidates, more than *eight times* as much. And, in 2018, women donated *more* money to female Democratic congressional candidates than to the men even as women accounted for less than one-third of all Democratic congressional candidates and just 43% of Democratic congressional nominees who ran in party primaries (Haley and Evers-Hillstrom 2019). What is even more remarkable is that in 2018 more than half of female Democrats who won their primaries (compared to just 39% of male Democrats) challenged Republican incumbents (CAWP 2019). This study confirms our understanding of what is means to be a WRPD—over successive election cycles and especially in 2018, when an

ROSALYN COOPERMAN

especially large group of female Democrats ran for Congress, female donors made clear their preference for progressive women and more representation by them. As such, it is even more important to examine the role played by women's PACs in the 2018 midterms.

EMILY's List Is *the* Liberal Women's PAC

Women's PACs were borne of a frustration with *both parties'* lackluster efforts to recruit women to run in competitive contests and not as sacrificial lambs in hopeless contests against entrenched incumbents. EMILY's List, formed in 1986 to elect pro-choice Democratic female candidates, is not the oldest women's PAC with member WRPDs, but it is the largest in the sheer volume of money raised on their behalf. Indeed, two decades prior, in 1966, NOW began endorsing and raising money for any female (and select male) candidates who supported a pro-ERA platform regardless of whether it was likely they would be elected. For its part, NOW continues to endorse and make modest contributions to pro-choice candidates but has redirected much of its energies toward community activism. (See Burrell 1994 and Cooperman 2010 for a history of women's PACs.)

In contrast to the first group of women's PACs that gave money to nearly any progressive woman who wanted to run for Congress, EMILY's List has always been selective in deciding on which women merit its assistance. Specifically, it requires that Democratic female candidates meet two conditions to receive the group's endorsement: they must prove viability with a demonstrated capacity to independently raise funds, and they must identify as pro-choice. A key factor that distinguishes EMILY's List from other PACs is its practice of directing funds to endorsed candidates early in the election cycle, often during a primary and even when that primary is a contested one. This strategy is especially important because it allows for women to signal viability and use the endorsement to raise funds from group members in both the primary and the general elections (Pimlott 2010). EMILY's List does not endorse or raise money for male Democrats, and will even direct funds to oppose them if they are running in a primary featuring an endorsed female candidate. EMILY's List also pioneered the use of bundling smaller funds from individual members to endorsed candidates, a fundraising technique now widely used by most PACs (Pimlott 2010).

Beginning in the 2010 election cycle EMILY's List expanded the reach of its organization and formed a super PAC, WomenVote! to raise unlimited amounts of funds called independent expenditures to advocate for the election or defeat of identified candidates. Federal campaign-finance laws allow an organization that has a traditional PAC to also establish a super PAC. The traditional PAC raises funds from members and then distributes those funds to political parties or candidate campaigns. Super PACs do not make these types of contributions but may raise unlimited amounts of funds from members to engage in electioneering activities independent of parties or campaigns. And, a group that has a PAC and a super PAC can lawfully engage in these activities as long as they disclose the source of contributions exceeding $200 in an election and also establish and maintain separate funding structures to collect and spend the funds (FEC 2014).

As noted on its website, EMILY's List has also developed programs to facilitate Democratic women's political candidacy beyond monetary contributions. Its Run to Win program provides campaign training to prospective and new candidates, and its Political Opportunity Project (POP) develops women's candidacies at the state and local level and in doing so creates a pipeline for pro-choice female Democrats who may run for Congress at a later date (EMILY's List 2019). In sum, over many years EMILY's List has developed the equivalent of one-stop shopping for progressive Democratic female candidates. It has a candidate-training program that demystifies the process for those interested in running for office. It has a pipeline program that nurtures local and state Democratic female officeholders and encourages their progressive ambition to run for national or statewide office. It has a traditional PAC that endorses competitive female candidates and bundles member funds to them early in their candidacies to maximize fundraising opportunities in primary and general elections. And it has a super PAC that raises and spends unlimited amounts of money to help elect an endorsed candidate facing a particularly competitive election. EMILY's List is the only women's PAC that offers female candidates access to a series of programs at every stage of a candidacy. The catch, of course, is that these services are only available to progressive women endorsed by the group.

The 2018 midterm election cycle was a particularly active one for EMILY's List as it endorsed fifty-five US House and twelve US Senate female candidates.[3] All of the candidates EMILY's List endorsed were women, and all of the funds raised and distributed assisted women. In the 2018 congressional election cycle EMILY's List and its super PAC, WomenVote! raised and distributed more than $100 million dollars to support Democratic female candidates. This amount is even more remarkable in the context of its efforts in 2016 when it endorsed Hillary Clinton as the Democratic Party presidential nominee and raised funds for Clinton and Democratic women congressional candidates.[4] Table 4.1 summarizes EMILY's List PAC campaign finance activities for 2018 and shows how many female Democrats the PAC endorsed as well as the amount of money raised (receipts) and spent (disbursements) on behalf of endorsed candidates.

Table 4.1 Campaign Finance Activities for Selected Women's PACs, 2018 Elections

Group	Endorsement Criteria	# women endorsed (House/Senate)	Receipts	Disbursements
EMILY's List	Viable, pro-choice Democratic woman	55/12	$61,713,282	$62,931,825
Susan B. Anthony List	Pro-life candidates for Congress and high state public office*	26 (of 64 total)/ 6 (of 15 total)	$697,925	$704,763
VIEW PAC	Qualified, viable Republican women congressional candidates	42/8	$1,860,870	$947,807
Winning for Women	Free-market conservative women running for federal office	9/3	$495,475	$489,076

SOURCE: Center for Responsive Politics summaries of PAC campaign-finance reports filed with the Federal Election Commission, endorsement totals compiled by author from PAC websites.

* The Susan B. Anthony List endorses both male and female pro-life candidates, so the total number reflects all candidates the group endorsed.

The shared goal of conservative women's PACs, formed as a counterweight to EMILY's List, has been to adopt some of the strategies employed by EMILY's List but in service to Republican female candidates. The Susan B. Anthony List was formed in 1992 to "end abortion by electing national leaders and advocating for laws that save lives, with a special calling to promote pro-life women leaders."[5] And, like EMILY's List, it maintains endorsement criteria that explicitly reference a candidate's position on abortion, but from a pro-life perspective. Other conservative women's PACs were formed to elect Republican women and emphasized different endorsement criteria. As stated on their respective websites, VIEW PAC was formed in 1997 to elect "viable Republican women to Congress,"[6] and Winning for Women was formed in 2017 to "support free-market conservative women running for federal office."[7] Neither of the latter two groups explicitly identifies a particular stance on abortion as a criterion for endorsement. Neither VIEW PAC nor the Susan B. Anthony List offers candidate-training programs; Winning for Women has a page on its website to identify prospective female candidates. All three conservative women's PACs endorse candidates and bundle member funds on their behalf. However, these conservative women's PACs do not typically endorse or raise money for Republican female candidates in their primaries but instead wait until after they have secured their party's nomination. Withholding these funds until after a primary victory is a problem because it is precisely at that juncture where female Republicans acutely need those resources (Shames 2015).

The Susan B. Anthony List and Winning for Women are traditional PACs that contribute funds directly to candidates' campaigns. VIEW PAC is identified by the Center for Responsive Politics as a "Carey Committee," a hybrid PAC that is both a traditional PAC but also a PAC that raises and distributes independent expenditures through a separate account (Center for Responsive Politics 2019). Like EMILY's List's WomenVote! the Susan B. Anthony List also has a super PAC, called Women Speak Out, which has raised independent expenditures since 2012. The Susan B. Anthony List Candidate Fund "finances and endorses pro-life candidates for congress and high state public office."[8] The Women Speak Out PAC identifies itself as a "superPAC amplifying the voices of women opposed to abortion extremists in Congress."[9] In practice, both of these entities affiliated with the Susan B. Anthony List give money to male and female pro-life candidates. In other words, Republican male and female candidates essentially compete with one another for endorsements and funding from these two PACs. Neither VIEW PAC nor Winning for Women endorses or contributes funds to male Republicans.

In 2018, conservative women's PACs varied widely in the number of candidates they endorsed, how many of the endorsed candidates were men, and the funds raised (receipts) and distributed (disbursements) on their behalf. However, as table 4.1 indicates, these PACs endorsed fewer candidates and also raised and spent significantly less money for endorsed candidates when compared to EMILY's List. Recall that EMILY's List endorses only Democratic female candidates based on an embrace of a pro-choice position and a demonstrated capacity to independently fundraise. As noted in table 4.1, conservative women's PACs each have different criteria for endorsement, and many of the female Republicans endorsed by these groups (specifically the Susan B. Anthony List and VIEW PAC) were incumbents running for reelection. VIEW PAC endorsed 42 and 8 Republican female candidates for the House and Senate, respectively, and raised and distributed nearly $3 million dollars for these candidates. Winning for Women, in its first election cycle, endorsed 9 and 3 Republican female candidates for the House and Senate, respectively, and raised and distributed about $500,000 for these candidates. The Susan B. Anthony List Candidate Fund endorsed 64 pro-life House candidates (26 of them female Republicans) and 15 pro-life Senate candidates (6 of them female Republicans). Put another way, a majority of the candidates endorsed by the Susan B. Anthony List Candidate Fund were male Republicans. Along with its super PAC, Women Speak Out, the two affiliated PACs raised and distributed nearly $3 million dollars to support female Republicans.[10] This endorsement means that male and female Republicans competed with one another for Susan B. Anthony List member–bundled contributions and other resources.

There are two important takeaways from table 4.1—how much money was raised and spent and which candidates were endorsed. First, the three conservative women's PACs combined raised and distributed *less than one tenth* the amount of money raised and distributed by EMILY's List. These funds are not inconsequential but pale in comparison to the fundraising might of EMILY's List. Conservative women's PACs provide smaller amounts of monetary support to endorsed candidates. Second, conservative women's PACs endorse fewer candidates, some of whom are men and many of whom are incumbents, not challengers or candidates for open seats. And, in the case of the Susan B. Anthony List, fewer than half of those congressional candidates endorsed in 2018 were female Republicans, which also means that only a portion of funds went to Republican female candidates. Less money *and* more competition with male Republican candidates for these funds therefore act as a double strike against female Republican candidates.

An analysis of Carol Miller's (R-WV) campaign-finance records shows how conservative women's PACs should embrace viable female Republican candidates. Miller ran for and won an open seat in West Virginia's Third Congressional District, a seat that was previously held by a Republican, and emerged as the only female Republican newly elected in 2018. The Cook Political Report classified the race as "lean Republican" (Wasserman 2018), which indicated that Republicans were likely to hold onto the seat. The Susan B. Anthony List, VIEW PAC, and Winning for Women each endorsed Miller in her contested primary and contributed the maximum allowable direct PAC contribution of $5,000. VIEW PAC and Winning for Women again contributed $5,000 to Miller's campaign for the general election; the Susan B. Anthony List contributed $1,000 to Miller for the general election.[11] All three PACs bundled member-contribution funds for Miller. Carol Miller won a plurality of the vote in her primary against five other Republicans and won the general election with 56% of the vote (Ballotpedia 2018).The early endorsement and financial support conservative women's PACs gave Miller during her contested primary came when Miller needed that support the most. It helped her emerge victorious from the primary, which allowed her to compete in the general election in a seat that was rated as winnable for Republicans.

Female Republicans Also Compete for Independent Expenditures

The disparity in funding available to House Democratic and Republican female candidates expands even further in 2018 when examining independent expenditure (IE) totals for these PACs. Federal campaign-finance

ROSALYN COOPERMAN

regulations allow for PACs to raise and spend unlimited amounts of money in IEs to support or oppose a candidate as long they do not contribute directly to a candidate's campaign, disclose the source of IE contributions, and do not coordinate their messaging and electioneering efforts with a candidate's campaign (FEC 2014). Typically, IEs target competitive contests in winnable open seats or against vulnerable incumbents. Independent expenditures are most frequently used for campaign advertising and messaging and may call for the defeat or election of a specified candidate. And, at least when looking at WomenVote! and Women Speak Out IE funds, a majority of the funds are directed to negative messaging against a candidate running against a candidate the PAC has endorsed (Cooperman and Crowder-Meyer 2018).

Table 4.2 lists the independent expenditure activity of EMILY's List WomenVote! and Susan B. Anthony List Women Speak Out, as these two super PACs raised the largest amounts of IE funds in the 2018 elections. The contrast in where these two super PACs directed funds is particularly relevant and indicates the funding advantages enjoyed by Democratic female candidates endorsed by EMILY's List and the challenges facing Republican female candidates and conservative women's PACs. The impact of IE funds from the other two conservative women's PACs, VIEW PAC and Winning for Women, bear only a brief mention as they were either ineffectual or too modest.

According to campaign-finance reports, VIEW PAC spent nearly a million dollars ($947,807) in IE funds in 2018, but the entirety of that amount was spent on behalf of one candidate, Republican Amie Hoeber—a former undersecretary of the Army during the Reagan administration—who ran for the open seat in Maryland's Sixth Congressional District.[12] While Hoeber's previous political experience made her an attractive candidate, the decision to direct close to a million dollars in IE funds to this contest was a curious one as the seat was characterized as a relatively "safe" Democratic seat by the Cook Political Report in its ratings of 2018 House contests (Wasserman 2018). Indeed, the Democratic candidate in the race, David Trone, soundly defeated Hoeber in the general election by a 59 to 38% margin.[13] For its part, Winning for Women (in its first election cycle) spent significantly less—just over $14,000 in IE funds—in 2018 and generally on positive messaging for about a dozen Republican female candidates in both the House and Senate with an average IE expenditure of about $1,000.[14]

Table 4.2 Independent Expenditures for WomenVote! and Women Speak Out, 2018

WomenVote! Independent Expenditures (IE)		Women Speak Out Independent Expenditures (IE)	
Overall IE total (House and Senate races)	$28,022,490	Overall IE total (House and Senate races)	$1,328,654
IE against—House (Rep women, n = 5)	$1,796,797	IE against—House (Dem women, n = 1)	$2,500
IE against—House (Rep men, n = 19)	$8,963,390	IE against—House (Dem men, n = 3)	$31,270
IE against—House (Dem men, n = 4)	$641,198	IE for—House (Rep women, n = 1)	$2,500
IE for—House (Dem women, n = 28)	$8,899,357	IE for—House (Rep men, n = 4)	$31,270
IE against—Senate (Rep women, n = 1)	$1,091,325	IE against—Senate (Dem women, n = 5)	$423,104
IE against—Senate (Rep men, n = 2)	$6,113,093	IE against—Senate (Dem men, n = 5)	$380,562
IE for—Senate (Dem women, n = 2)	$517,330	IE for—Senate (Rep women, n = 4)	$254,214
IE for or against—Senate (Dem men, n = 0)	$0	IE for—Senate (Rep men, n = 6)	$203,234

Note: WomenVote! is the super PAC affiliated with EMILY's List; Women Speak Out is the super PAC affiliated with the Susan B. Anthony List. Expenditure totals were compiled by author from Center for Responsive Politics data and PAC campaign-finance reports filed with the FEC.

In 2018, EMILY's List WomenVote! spent over $28 million on IE funds with the majority of those funds, over $20 million, directed to twenty-eight House races featuring Democratic female candidates, the majority of whom were challengers running against male Republican incumbents.[15] It allocated the remaining amount, about $7 million, on two Senate contests—a challenge to Missouri incumbent Claire McCaskill and a challenge from

ROSALYN COOPERMAN

Rep. Jacky Rosen to incumbent Senator Dean Heller in Nevada. (The outcome was mixed—McCaskill lost her reelection bid; Rosen won the open seat). EMILY's List spent all of its funds on contests featuring Democratic female candidates and even spent about $640,000 in IE funds directed to primaries against Democratic men candidates.[16] It spent zero IE funds on House or Senate contests in support of Democratic men candidates. The decision of EMILY's List WomenVote! to direct IE funds to competitive House contests was strategically sound as Democrats flipped enough House seats in 2018, many of them by women, to secure a party majority in the chamber.

By comparison, Susan B. Anthony List Women Speak Out directed its IE funds differently even as it raised significantly less money than EMILY's List WomenVote! Women Speak Out directed most of its funds—over $1.2 million of the $1.3 million total—to Senate contests, which was a smart strategy as Republicans not only maintained, but expanded, their Senate majority. On the Senate side, Women Speak Out directed over $250,000 in IE funds in support of four Senate races with Republican female candidates and over $200,000 in support of six Senate races with Republican men candidates (with four of those contests featuring only men candidates).[17] In other words, Republican male and female Senate candidates were about equally likely to have Women Speak Out spend IE funds to support their Senate elections. On the House side, Women Speak Out allocated about $70,000 in IE funds to House contests but directed those funds in support of only one female Republican, Rep. Virginia Foxx, and four male Republicans (three of whom were running against male Democrats).[18] When looking at the allocation of IE funds by Women Speak Out, it is clear that Republican female candidates competed with male Republicans for IE funds from this conservative women's PAC. In contrast, Democratic female candidates were the only beneficiaries of IE funds raised by EMILY's List WomenVote! Not only do Republican female candidates have less access to IE funds from conservative women's PACs, Republican female candidates must also compete for those resources with the men in their party. By contrast, Democratic female candidates have access to significantly larger amounts of IE funds and do not have to compete with campaigns of male Democrats to have those IE funds directed their way.

In sum, the campaign-finance activity of liberal and conservative women's PACs makes clear that 2018 was a very strong year for female

Democratic candidates, many of whom received substantial financial support from sources simply not available to Republican female candidates. Female donors directed a majority of their funds to female Democrats, and EMILY's List and its super PAC, WomenVote! raised millions of additional dollars to elect more progressive women to Congress. The reverse would prove to be true for Republicans. Conservative women's PACs raised significantly less money to contribute to their campaigns and typically contributed funds only in the general, not primary, elections. And, in the case of the Susan B. Anthony List, Republican female candidates had to compete with the men from their party for those funds. These realities make navigating the campaign-finance network on the House side easier and more beneficial for Democratic female candidates and more challenging and less rewarding for Republican female candidates.

On the House side, EMILY's List helped Democratic female candidates maximize their electoral opportunities. According to CAWP, all 54 Democratic female incumbents who ran were returned to office, 20 female Democrats won open seats, and 15 female Democrats defeated incumbents, the majority of whom were male Republicans. Together, 89 female Democrats serve as US representatives in the 116th Congress, a record number. Republican women fared poorly by comparison, and conservative women's PACs remained at the margins of efforts to assist them. Five of the 17 female Republican incumbents who ran for reelection were defeated, and only one female Republican won an open seat. No female Republican challengers defeated incumbents in 2018 (CAWP 2019). As such, the number of female Republicans serving as US representatives in the 116th Congress actually *decreased* by 10 to just 13 members; thus there are more than *five times* as many women House Democrats as House Republicans.

Conservative women's PACs fared a bit better in their efforts to elect Republican female Senate candidates in 2018 though the party gap between women Republican and Democratic senators did not improve as they continue to be outnumbered by more than two to one (17 to 8). As noted by CAWP, 10 women Senators were not up for reelection in 2018. Nine of 11 female Democratic incumbent senators won reelection, and 2 female Democrats were newly elected as senators—one who defeated an incumbent and another who won an open seat. Both female Republican incumbents won reelection, and 3 new female Republicans joined the Senate, 1 who defeated an incumbent, another who won election in a run-off, and a third who was appointed to fill the vacancy of a deceased Republican incumbent (CAWP 2019).

Women's PACs, Female Candidates, and Future Congressional Elections

Looking forward, future elections will bring challenges and opportunities to Democratic and Republican female candidates and the liberal and conservative women's PACs that endorse them and raise money to support their elections. In 2020, Democrats will seek to retain, if not expand, their Democratic majority in the House and flip majority party control of the Senate, which is possible as Republicans have more Senate seats to defend this cycle. Democrats will work to maintain the momentum of the 2018 congressional midterms and defeat the incumbent Republican at the top of the ticket, President Donald Trump. To that end several women officeholders (many of whom are EMILY's List alumna) are running for the Democratic presidential nomination to take on Trump directly. Of course, Republicans will seek to improve, if not strengthen, their own positions in expanding their majority in the Senate, retaking the House, and securing the reelection of President Trump.

For their part, women's PACs are also sizing up the 2020 elections and their places in it. Already, women's PACs are laying out their strategies to protect, if not expand, the number of female candidates from their preferred party and engaging directly with one another in the process. By March 2019, less than two months after the 116th Congress had convened, EMILY's List posted its "2020 Targets List" that included 43 House and 6 Senate Republicans whose seats were being targeted by the group, with 5 women Republican representatives (including Rep. Elise Stefanik and the National Republican Congressional Committee recruitment chair, Rep. Susan Brooks) and 2 women Republican senators named to the list. Not surprisingly, this move by EMILY's List drew sharp criticism from Winning for Women, who decried, "For a group that claims to empower women, EMILY's List is already targeting five of the just 13 Republican women in the House."[19] At that same time EMILY's List announced it had endorsed 2 female Democratic incumbent senators and 25 female Democratic incumbent representatives for reelection (EMILY's List 2019).

At a time when candidates (and prospective candidates) on both side of the aisle are weighing reelection and election bids, EMILY's List has already begun raising money to aid the reelection of nearly 30 female Democratic congressional candidates ahead of any party primaries they may face. The group also signaled its intention to make the reelection bids of nearly 50 Republican members of Congress (including 7 women) more contentious and certainly more costly. And, in at least one case to date, EMILY's List might well take credit for forcing the hand of one Republican incumbent they targeted, Susan Brooks (R-IN), who announced in June 2019 that she would not run for reelection in 2020. The loss of Representative Brooks is a double hit for Republicans as they must find another candidate to defend her now-open seat and also fill her position as NRCC candidate-recruitment chair. Her retirement also hurts women in the party as Representative Brooks, like Representative Stefanik, worked especially hard to recruit women Republicans to Congress. Early in the 2020 season, EMILY's List released its shot across the bow that put Republicans and conservative women's PACs on the defensive, and they are raising money to make good on those plans. At the end of the first fundraising quarter, EMILY's List and its super PAC, WomenVote! have already raised more than $16 million for the 2020 election cycle.[20]

Aside from criticizing EMILY's List for its activities, conservative women's PACs have been slower to get moving on the swiftly approaching 2020 elections. The Susan B. Anthony List has thus far endorsed 2 women House candidates. At the end of the first fundraising quarter, the group and its super PAC, Women Speak Out, have raised over $500,000 for the 2020 election cycle.[21] VIEW PAC has endorsed all of the female Republican incumbents running for reelection and has raised about $300,000 in the first fundraising quarter for 2020.[22] Winning for Women, at least in word, if not deed, has recognized that Republican female candidates need help from women's PACs like them. It announced the creation of a super PAC, WFW Action Fund, and a goal of electing 20 Republican women in 2020 (Schuller 2019). At the end of the first fundraising quarter, however, the PAC had raised just over $100,000 for 2020.[23]

And what of Representative Elise Stefanik, who made a similar promise to "play big" in primaries in 2020 to support Republican female candidates? Despite her tenure as a recruiter for House Republicans, Stefanik's own record of fundraising is more modest. According to the Center for Responsive Politics, in 2018 Stefanik's leadership PAC raised over $300,000 for her PAC and distributed $129,000 in contributions to Republican candidates.[24] A few months into the start of the 116th Congress, Stefanik launched her rebranded leadership PAC, E-PAC, "to engage, empower, elevate, and elect Republican women to Congress."[25] The website identifies 15 women Republican incumbents as "women leaders" and maintains a separate page for donations. To date, however, E-PAC has not filed any campaign-finance reports for the 2020 election cycle with the Federal Election Commission. Stefanik's own reelection committee, Elise for Congress, lists about $900,000 in receipts in a campaign-finance report filed with the FEC in the first quarter of the 2020 election cycle.[26] Also recall that Stefanik's House seat was one of the seats EMILY's List announced it was targeting in 2020. Thus, for Representative Stefanik, who pledged to expand the number of Republican female candidates to Congress, she may well need to include her own seat in her ambitious fundraising plans to close the party gap in representation between Democratic and Republican women officeholders.

Notes

1. National Republican Congressional Committee, June 25, 2018, "NRCC Recruitment Chair Elise Stefanik: We Must Encourage Non-Traditional Candidates to Run," NRCC Press Update, www.nrcc.org/2018/06/25/nrcc-recruitment-chair-elise-stefanik-must-encourage -non-traditional-candidates-run/.

2. CAWP 2019, "Women Candidates 1992–2018: A Summary of Major Party Primary Candidates for U.S. Senate, U.S. House."

3. Figures compiled by author from EMILY's List press releases announcing candidate endorsements.

4. Figures compiled by author from campaign-finance reports filed with the Federal Election Commission for 2016 and 2018.

5. "About Susan B. Anthony List," www.sba-list.org/about-susan-b-anthony-list.

6. "About VIEW PAC," viewpac.org/about/.

7. "Our Mission: Winning for Women," winningforwomen.com/about-us/.

8. "Mission: Susan B. Anthony List Candidate Fund," www.sba-list.org/candidate-fund.

9. "About: Women Speak Out PAC," www.sba-list.org/women-speak-out-pac.

10. Center for Responsive Politics summaries of PAC campaign-finance reports filed with the Federal Election Commission, endorsement totals compiled by author from PAC websites.

11. Author analysis of candidate and PAC campaign finance reports filed in 2018 with the FEC.

12. Open Secrets 2018, "VIEW PAC, Summary." www.opensecrets.org/pacs/indexpend .php?cycle=2018&cmte=C00327189.

13. Ballotpedia 2019, "Maryland's 6th Congressional District Election, 2018." ballotpedia
.org/Maryland%27s_6th_Congressional_District_election, 2018.

14. Open Secrets 2018, "Winning for Women, Summary." www.opensecrets.org/pacs/look
up2.php?strID=C00646703&cycle=2018.

15. Totals compiled by author from EMILY's List press releases and campaign finance
reports filed with the FEC.

16. Open Secrets 2018, "WomenVote!, Summary," www.opensecrets.org/pacs/lookup2
.php?strID=C00473918.

17. Open Secrets 2018, "Women Speak Out, Summary."

18. Open Secrets 2018, "Women Speak Out, Summary."

19. Winning for Women, March 1, 2019, "WFW Statement on 2020 Targets Named by
EMILY's List," *Winning for Women,* winningforwomen.com/wfw-statement-on-2020-targets
-named-by-emilys-list/.

20. Totals compiled by author from campaign finance reports filed through June 30,
2019, with the FEC.

21. Totals compiled by author from campaign finance reports filed through June 30,
2019, with the FEC.

22. Totals compiled by author from campaign finance reports filed through June 30,
2019, with the FEC.

23. Totals compiled by author from campaign finance reports filed through June 30,
2019, with the FEC.

24. Open Secrets 2019, "Elise Stefanik Leadership PAC, Summary," www.opensecrets.org
/members-of-congress/summary?cid=N00035523&cycle=2018&type=P.

25. "E-PAC: About," elevate-pac.com/about/.

26. Elise for Congress, campaign-finance return through June 30, 2019, filed with the
FEC, www.fec.gov/data/committee/C00547893/.

References

Ballotpedia. 2018. "Carol Miller (West Virginia)." ballotpedia.org/Carol_Miller
_(West_Virginia).

Biersack, Robert, Paul S. Herrnson, and Clyde Wilcox. 1994. *Risky Business? PAC
Decisionmaking in Congressional Elections.* New York: Routledge.

Bryner, Sarah, and Doug Weber. 2013. "Sex, Money & Politics." *Center for Responsive Politics.* www.opensecrets.org/news/reports/sex-money-politics.

Burrell, Barbara. 1994. *A Woman's Place Is in the House: Campaigning for Congress
in the Feminist Era.* Ann Arbor: University of Michigan Press.

Carroll, Susan J., and Kira Sanbonmatsu. 2013. *More Women Can Run: Gender and
Pathways to the State Legislatures.* New York: Oxford University Press.

CAWP. 29 November 2018. "Results: Women Candidates in the 2018 Elections." cawp
.rutgers.edu/sites/default/files/resources/results_release_5bletterhead5d_1.pdf.

———. 2019. "Women Candidates, 1992–2018: A Summary of Major Party Primary Candidates for U.S. Senate, U.S. House." Center for American Women

in Politics. cawp.rutgers.edu/sites/default/files/resources/canprimcong_hist sum.pdf.

Center for Responsive Politics. 2019. "Types of Advocacy Groups." www.opensecrets .org/527s/types.php.

Cooperman, Rosalyn. 2010. "EMILY's Friends: The Emerging Relationship between EMILY's List, Organized Labor, and Women Candidates in U.S. House Elections, 2002–2008." Presented at the annual meeting of the American Political Science Association, Washington, DC.

Cooperman, Rosalyn, and Melody Crowder-Meyer. 2018. "A Run for Their Money: Republican Women's Hard Road to Campaign Funding," in *The Right Women: Republican Party Activists, Candidates, and Legislators,* ed. Malliga Och and Shauna Shames. Santa Barbara, CA: Praeger.

Crespin, Michael H., and Janna L. Deitz. 2010. "If You Can't Join 'Em, Beat 'Em: The Gender Gap in Individual Donations to Congressional Candidates." *Political Research Quarterly* 63 (3): 581–93.

Crowder-Meyer, Melody, and Rosalyn Cooperman. 2018. "Can't Buy Them Love: How Party Culture among Donors Contributes to the Party Gap in Women's Representation." *Journal of Politics* 80 (4): 1211–24.

Dittmar, Kelly. 2015. *Navigating Gendered Terrain: Stereotypes and Strategy in Political Campaigns.* Philadelphia: Temple University Press.

Dittmar, Kelly, Kira Sanbonmatsu, and Susan J. Carroll. 2018. *A Seat at the Table: Congresswomen's Perspectives on Why Their Presence Matters.* New York: Oxford University Press.

EMILY's List. 2019. "Run to Win." emilyslist.org/run-to-win.

FEC. June 2014. "Federal Election Commission Campaign Guide: Congressional Candidates and Committees." www.fec.gov/resources/cms-content/documents /candgui.pdf.

Haley, Grace, and Karl Evers-Hillstrom. February 22, 2019. "State of Money in Politics: Female Donors Gaining Influence as 2020 Kicks Off." *Center for Responsive Politics.* www.opensecrets.org/news/2019/02/somp4-female-donors-gaining -influence-as-2020-kicks/.

Hannagan, Rebecca J., Jamie P. Pimlott, and Levente Littvay. 2010. "Does an EMILY's List Endorsement Predict Electoral Success, or Does EMILY Pick the Winners?" *P.S.: Political Science & Politics* 43 (3): 503–8.

Jacobson, Gary C. 1981. *Strategy and Choice in Congressional Elections.* New Haven, CT: Yale University Press.

Jenkins, Jeffrey A. 2007. "Negative Agenda Control in the Senate and House: Fingerprints of Majority Party Power." *Journal of Politics* 69 (3): 689–700.

Kim, Henry A., and Brad L LeVeck. 2013. "Money, Reputation, and Incumbency in U.S. House Elections, or Why Marginals Have Become More Expensive." *American Political Science Review* 107 (3): 492–504.

Kitchens, Karin E., and Michele L. Swers. 2016. "Why Aren't There More Republican Women in Congress? Gender, Partisanship, and Fundraising Support in the 2010 and 2012 Elections." *Politics & Gender* 12 (4): 648–76.

Lawless, Jennifer L., and Richard L. Fox. 2010. *It Still Takes a Candidate: Why Women Don't Run for Office.* Cambridge, UK: Cambridge University Press.

Open Secrets 2018. "Women Speak Out, Summary." www.opensecrets.org/pacs /lookup2.php?strID=C00530766.

Pager, Tyler. December 20, 2018. "After Big Losses, a N.Y. House Republican Clashes with Her Party." *New York Times.* www.nytimes.com/2018/12/20/ny region/elise-stefanik-republican-women.html.

Pathe, Simone. December 4, 2018. "Elise Stefanik Wants to Play in Primaries to Help Republican Women." *Roll Call.* www.rollcall.com/news/politics/elise -stefanik-wants-to-play-in-primaries-to-help-republican-women.

Pimlott, Jamie Pamelia. 2010. *Women and the Democratic Party: The Evolution of EMILY's List.* Amherst, NY: Cambria.

Schuller, Rebecca. June 19, 2019. "2020 can be the year of the Republican woman— but it will take work." *The Hill.* thehill.com/blogs/congress-blog/politics/449165 -2020-can-be-the-year-of-the-republican-woman-but-it-will-take?rnd=1560 889128.

Shames, Shauna. 2015. "The GOP Gender Gap: Clearing the Primary Hurdles." Political Parity, Hunt Alternative Funds. www.politicalparity.org/wp-content /uploads/2018/07/primary-hurdles-full-report.pdf.

Thomsen, Danielle M., and Michele L. Swers. 2017. "Which Women Can Run? Gender, Partisanship, and Candidate Donor Networks." *Political Research Quarterly* 70 (2): 449–63.

Wasserman, David. November 5, 2018. "Final House Ratings: 75 Competitive Races, Ten Rating Changes." *Cook Political Report.*

VOTING FOR
WOMEN

USING GENDER AND PARTISAN STEREOTYPES TO EVALUATE FEMALE CANDIDATES

SYLVIA I. GONZALEZ AND NICHOLE M. BAUER

Postmortems of the 2016 electoral outcome debate the extent to which gender bias contributed to Hillary Clinton's historic presidential defeat (Bracic, Israel-Trummel, and Shortle 2019; Cassese and Holman 2019; Valentino, Wayne, and Oceno 2018). Perceptions of a female candidate's personality traits can lead to bias if voters see female candidates as having feminine traits and lacking the masculine qualities associated with political leaders (Huddy and Terkildsen 1993; Bauer 2015a; Ditonto 2017). An alternative perspective argues that Hillary Clinton lost the election due to partisanship. Voters frequently use candidate partisanship to infer that female candidates have traits that reinforce stereotypes about the political parties (Rahn 1993; Hayes 2005). Parsing the influence of gender and partisan stereotypes is challenging because the content of these two stereotypes overlap with one another (Winter 2010; Hayes 2011).

Extant scholarship identifies three types of stereotypes voters apply to female candidates. First, a gender-driven model argues that voters attribute to female candidates qualities that reinforce feminine stereotypes, and this association reduces electoral support (Huddy and Terkildsen 1993). Second, under a partisan-driven model, voters use partisan heuristics to infer that candidates have qualities that reflect the appropriate partisan stereotype (Rahn 1993; Petrocik 1996; Hayes 2005). The third model, the interactive stereotype model, posits that gender and partisan stereotypes can, for some candidates, combine so that voters see Democratic female candidates as having more feminine qualities than co-partisan male candidates because partisan and gender stereotypes reinforce one another (Sanbonmatsu and Dolan 2009; Schneider and Bos 2016; Bauer 2018; Hayes 2011). These three models lead to very different conclusions about the role of gender stereotypes in voter decision-making, and the current scholarship offers no clear consensus on how gender stereotypes affect voter decision-making.

Voters frequently use all three models of stereotyping in politics to evaluate female candidates; we develop a framework to explain how and when voters use a gender, partisan, or interactive stereotype model. Voters use different models of gender and partisan stereotypes to evaluate candidates based on both candidate sex and candidate partisanship. Voters do not use just one stereotype to evaluate female candidates but rather shift between gender, partisan, or a combination of the two to form impressions of female candidates.

Models of Stereotyping Female Candidates

Feminine stereotypes characterize women as caring, sensitive, and nurturing—qualities that reflect the communal, or more supportive, social roles held by women (Eagly and Karau 2002). Masculine stereotypes characterize men as strong, aggressive, and decisive—qualities that reflect the agentic, or more powerful, social roles held by men, which include positions of political leadership (Huddy and Terkildsen 1993; Conroy 2015). Gender stereotypes also shape the stereotypes voters hold of the political parties. Voters associate the Democratic Party with feminine traits while voters associate the Republican Party with masculine traits (Winter 2010). Extant scholarship finds evidence for three models that voters use to form impressions of female political candidates: the gender stereotyping model, the partisan stereotyping model, and the interactive gender and partisan model.

Feminine stereotypes can undermine electoral support for female candidates because such qualities do not fit the masculine expectations voters hold for political leaders (Rosenwasser and Seale 1988; Alexander and Anderson 1993). Recent evidence suggests that voters do not associate female candidates with traits associated with feminine stereotypes (Bauer 2015b; Brooks 2013; Dolan 2014). Campaign strategies that reinforce feminine traits can, however, activate broader feminine stereotypes (Bauer 2015a) and undermine support for female candidates (Ditonto, Hamilton,

SYLVIA I. GONZALEZ AND NICHOLE M. BAUER

and Redlawsk 2014; Ditonto 2017). Feminine stereotypes can, under some conditions, benefit female candidates, but these benefits are highly contextual. For example, feminine stereotypes of women as ethical and honest can benefit female candidates running for office in the aftermath of a political scandal (Barnes and Beaulieu 2014). Current scholarship suggests that voters generally use feminine stereotypes to infer that female candidates lack the masculine qualities more frequently associated with political leadership.

Another approach argues that gender stereotypes are inconsequential because partisanship is such a dominant cue during campaigns (Dolan 2014). Evidence suggests that partisan stereotypes affect the trait competencies of Democratic female candidates (Sanbonmatsu and Dolan 2009; Hayes 2011), but the research offers mixed results on the influence of partisan stereotypes on issue and trait impressions of Republican female candidates (Bauer 2018; Hayes 2011; Koch 2001; Sanbonmatsu and Dolan 2009). The most prominent influence of partisanship is on vote-choice decisions where voters tend to select the candidate with whom they share partisanship. The role of partisan stereotypes is not clear under this model of candidate evaluation. Voters could select a Democratic or Republican female candidate *because* they associate this candidate with partisan stereotypes, or voters could select a female candidate *despite* gender stereotypes that do not comport with stereotypes of political leaders. The partisan-identity research suggests that voters will support candidates based on shared partisanship (Mason and Wronski 2018) even if voters see a female candidate as lacking the masculine traits voters desire in political leadership.

The third approach, the interactive stereotyping model, argues that voters simultaneously rely on both gender and partisan stereotypes. Voters more strongly associate Democratic female candidates with feminine traits and feminine issues compared to Democratic male candidates (Sanbonmatsu and Dolan 2009; Schneider and Bos 2016). This strong feminine trait and issue association suggests that *both* gender and partisan stereotypes affect Democratic female candidates. Voters do not associate Republican female candidates with the masculine traits and issues most consistent with partisan stereotypes (Bauer 2018). The interactive stereotyping model explains how voters form trait competencies of Democratic female candidates (Schneider and Bos 2016; Bauer 2018) but does not directly consider how the trait impressions voters form of a candidate affect voter decision-making. For example, Hayes (2011) finds that the partisan-consistent news coverage received by female candidates leads voters to associate female candidates with partisan-consistent traits; but this work does not analyze whether being associated with partisan-consistent traits depresses or bolsters support for Democratic and Republican female candidates.

Previous research assumes that voters use one, and only one, of these gender and partisan stereotype models to form impressions of female candidates. In other words, if voters use the partisan model to form impressions of the traits a candidate possesses, then voters will also use partisan stereotypes in vote-choice decisions. We argue that voters will shift between the gender, partisan, and interactive models. We investigate the influence of gender and partisan stereotypes through the lens of candidate traits because traits have the potential to pose as a source of bias that can limit the electoral effectiveness of female candidates. Cassese and Holman (2018) find that trait-based attacks against Democratic female candidates negatively affect voters while issue-based attacks leave these candidates relatively unscathed. Recent research finds that traits and issues operate differently for female compared to male candidates (Bauer 2019b), and this research builds on that work.

Constraining and Reinforcing Stereotypes

There are several possibilities for how gender stereotypes, partisan stereotypes, or a combination of these stereotypes affect traits voters attribute to female and male candidates, and how voters apply these traits to decision-making. We draw on two theories from psychology research. First, we turn to research on how individuals fit others into multiple stereotype categories to identify how gender and partisan stereotypes affect the traits voters attribute to candidates. Second, we use role-congruity theory to distinguish the effects of candidate traits on voter decision-making. Role-congruity theory argues that gender shapes the way individuals stereotype social roles, including political leadership roles, so that masculinity aligns with stereotypes about leaders while femininity is not congruent with stereotypes about leaders (Eagly and Karau 2002). To form our predictions about how voters apply traits to form impressions of candidates,

SYLVIA I. GONZALEZ AND NICHOLE M. BAUER

we examine recent research on the influence of partisan identities on the way voters form impressions about political candidates.

When individuals encounter others who fit into multiple stereotype categories, as is the case for most individuals, they will look for ways these cues overlap with and reinforce one another (Kunda and Thagard 1996). Overlapping stereotypes can reinforce one another to affect the traits attributed to a specific individual. Partisan and gender stereotypes can have a reinforcing effect for Democratic female candidates because the content of these two stereotypes fits together—voters stereotype Democrats as feminine and women with feminine qualities. A reinforcing relationship between gender and party stereotypes means that voters should see Democratic female candidates as having more feminine qualities relative to Democratic male candidates. A reinforcing trait-attribution model will also apply, we argue, to Republican male candidates, where voters will attribute them with masculine traits more strongly than Republican female candidates. Essentially, when gender and partisan stereotypes share overlapping content, individuals will combine the two stereotypes.

The underlying partisan and gender trait stereotypes about Republican female candidates conflict. There are several strategies voters can use to reconcile this conflict. Voters can add these two stereotypes together (Kunda and Thagard 1996). Under this model, voters will see candidates as having *both* gender and partisan stereotypic qualities. For instance, an additive model predicts that voters will associate Democratic male candidates with warmth, a partisan trait, and strength, a masculine trait. A second strategy for reconciling conflicting stereotypes is that one stereotype will constrain the power and meaning of the second stereotype (Biernat, Manis, and Nelson 1991). For example, a person may see a Democratic male candidate as being warm but may also see warmth as a negative quality because warmth does not fit into masculine stereotypes. It is likely that voters will use an additive model to infer the traits of a Democratic male candidate. Here, the congruity between being male and being a political leader will lead voters to add together gender and partisan stereotypes (Bos, Schneider, and Utz 2017). In other words, Democratic male candidates will benefit from the feminine stereotypes associated with their party and the masculine stereotypes associated with their sex to be seen as having both sets of gendered traits (Schneider and Bos 2016).

The literature offers unclear guidance on whether voters will add party and gender stereotypes for Republican female candidates or if party and gender stereotypes will constrain one another. Trait-attribution studies find that voters associate Republican female candidates with feminine traits and feminine issues (Bauer 2018; Hayes 2011; Koch 2001). Other studies find that voters attribute Republican female candidates with traits more consistent with partisan rather than gender stereotypes (Dolan 2014). Thus, it is possible that voters will attribute traits to Republican female candidates in an additive way (that is, these candidates will have feminine and masculine qualities) or a reinforcing way (these candidates will be seen as having neither feminine nor masculine qualities). There are two comparisons that lend insight into the reinforcing and constraining effects of multiple stereotypes. First, no differences within candidate partisanship but across candidate sex in the traits attributed to candidates indicate that partisan stereotypes hold sway over gender stereotypes—supporting a partisan- over a gender-driven model of evaluation. Second, no differences across candidate partisanship but within candidate sex (for example, comparing a Democratic female to a Republican female candidate) indicate that gender affects the influence of partisan stereotypes—indicating a gender-motivated over a partisan-motivated model.

The trait-attribution hypothesis delineates which stereotype-processing strategies will affect the traits ascribed to candidates.

Trait-Attribution Hypothesis

Gender and partisan stereotypes will reinforce one another for Democratic female and Republican male candidates while gender and partisan stereotypes will not have a reinforcing effect on Democratic male or Republican female candidates.

The ambiguity in the literature about how voters see Republican female candidates limits our ability to make a direct prediction about how voters will attribute traits to these candidates.

The trait-application hypothesis turns to identifying whether there are differences in how voters use traits to form impressions about candidates. Partisanship can serve as a protective shield for female candidates when they use gendered traits in their strategic campaign appeals. We develop

SYLVIA I. GONZALEZ AND NICHOLE M. BAUER

this argument from the literature on campaign strategies, which finds that voters frequently respond positively to candidates who emphasize issues and themes associated with their own political party (Riker 1996; Sides 2006; Simon 2002; Sulkin and Swigger 2008). Research extending this work on partisan appeals to how voters respond to differences across candidate sex finds that female candidates can benefit from a partisan-stereotypic strategy (Bauer 2019a). For example, voters may not respond negatively to a Democratic female candidate who emphasizes feminine traits because these are qualities that voters already attribute to Democratic women based on the combination of reinforcing partisan and gender stereotypes.

The idea of partisanship serving as protective cover for female candidates applies most strongly to Democratic female candidates because voters will be able to form more clear impressions of the traits these candidates possess due to the clear signals from gender and partisan stereotypes. Partisanship may not provide as much protective cover for Republican female candidates who are also emphasizing partisan stereotypic traits, in this case masculine traits. Emphasizing masculine traits has the potential to produce a counter-stereotypic backlash effect for Republican female candidates (Krupnikov and Bauer 2014), and it is possible voters will interpret masculine traits as *negative* or *undesirable* qualities in Republican women. For example, a Republican woman who emphasizes being tough may be seen as too tough and too aggressive and receive negative ratings because these qualities are undesirable in women more generally. This more negative evaluation comes from the more ambiguous trait-ownership impressions voters form of Republican female candidates based on the conflicting partisan- and gender-stereotypic signals.

The use of partisan traits that are also gendered traits will not have adverse effects for male candidates because male candidates do not need the protective shield, so to speak, provided by partisan stereotypes. Male candidates benefit from the association between their sex and masculine stereotypes and the association between masculine stereotypes and political leadership (Holman, Merolla, and Zechmeister 2016; Huddy and Terkildsen 1993). Thus, voters should always rate male candidates who emphasize partisan qualities positively. The trait-application hypothesis delineates how gender stereotypes will affect the way individuals evaluate the leadership abilities of candidates. The role of traits in these evaluations is that they are independent variables that affect broader assessments of candidate leadership ability and, ultimately, vote-choice decisions.

Trait-Application Hypothesis

Voters will use partisan stereotypes to evaluate Democratic female candidates who emphasize gendered partisan traits but will use gender stereotypes to evaluate Republican female candidates who emphasize gendered partisan traits.

The observable effects of the trait-application prediction are as follows. First, voters should rate a Democratic female and male candidate more positively when they emphasize partisan (feminine) traits compared to when they do not emphasize those traits. This means there may be no differences across candidate sex in voter responses to the partisan-trait strategies of Democratic female and male candidates. Second, voters should rate a Republican female candidate more negatively relative to a Republican male candidate when emphasizing partisan (masculine) traits compared to when they do not emphasize those traits.

Two Empirical Tests

Observational data from the American National Election Study (ANES) tests the trait-attribution prediction, using the actual traits attributed to female and male political candidates in House elections from 1992 to 2000. An original survey experiment with a nationally representative sample of US adults measures how voters respond to candidates of the same political party who emphasize traits that reinforce partisan stereotypes. With the observational data, we can measure the traits participants associate with actual, as opposed to hypothetical, female candidates. A limitation of the ANES data is that the survey stopped asking about House candidate traits in 2000. But the data collected when women became visible and high-profile political players allow us to capture the influence of gender and partisan stereotypes when the media and the public began to recognize women as major political players and as candidates, and to trace changes over five election cycles in the use of gender and partisan stereotypes to attribute traits to female candidates.

SYLVIA I. GONZALEZ AND NICHOLE M. BAUER

We start by examining the traits voters attribute to House candidates using the ANES open-ended House candidate likes and dislikes questions from 1992 through 2000. We use this time frame for both practical and strategic reasons. First, 1992 marked the "Year of the Woman," when candidate sex became a highly salient characteristic to many voters. We stop at the year 2000 simply because the ANES stopped asking the likes and dislikes questions about individual House candidates. The ANES preelection study allowed respondents to list up to five items they liked and disliked about Democratic and Republican House candidates in the respondent's district. Following Winter (2010), we coded the open-ended responses for the like and dislike responses into feminine and masculine traits. This set of feminine and masculine characteristics map onto *both* gender and partisanship stereotypes, and this overlap allows us to test the relationship between gender and partisan stereotypes in the impressions formed of female candidates. Feminine traits are partisan for Democrats while masculine traits are partisan for Republicans. We restricted the sample to include only respondents who listed at least one like or dislike about a Democratic or a Republican House candidate. We created feminine and masculine trait variables for the positive (likes) and negative (dislikes) attributions. We coded the variables as 1 if respondents listed a trait about a candidate and 0 otherwise.

To test the trait-attribution prediction, we estimated a series of probit models predicting the effect of candidate sex on listing a partisan trait about a candidate. We separated the models by candidate partisanship because differences between female and male candidates from the same political party suggest that gender stereotypes drive the traits voters attribute to candidates. Support for the trait-attribution hypothesis should produce the following observable results. First, respondents will be more likely to list a feminine trait about Democratic female candidates relative to Democratic male candidates. This difference indicates that gender and partisan stereotypes, which both include feminine traits, reinforce one another. Second, respondents should be more likely to list a masculine trait about a Republican male candidate relative to a Republican female candidate—again, this indicates that gender and party stereotypes reinforce one another. Third, we include the negative trait category because the influence of gender stereotypes on evaluations of Republican female candidates can emerge if voters see these qualities as negative qualities in women. Voters may view it as a negative if a Republican female candidate is aggressive but see that same quality as a positive in a Republican male candidate. Table 5.1 (see pages 104–105) reports the results.

There are no differences in the probability of listing a feminine trait about a Democratic female or Democratic male candidate. The absence of differences suggests that partisan stereotypes hold greater sway over voter trait attributions relative to gender stereotypes. This finding runs counter to the trait-attribution prediction. The theoretical expectation for Democratic male candidates is that gender and partisan stereotypes would have an additive effect so that participants attribute Democratic men with both feminine and masculine qualities. If an additive stereotype effect occurred, then respondents should be more likely to list a masculine trait about a Democratic male relative to a Democratic female candidate. The lack of differences across sex in the positive masculine traits attributed to Democratic candidates does not illustrate this pattern.[1] This first set of results suggest that partisan stereotypes play a dominant role in the traits attributed to Democratic candidates.

In the Republican models, several key patterns emerge. First, participants were equally likely to list a positive masculine trait about a Republican female candidate relative to a Republican male candidate. A reinforcing-stereotype relationship for Republican male candidates should have led participants to be *more* likely to attribute the Republican male with masculine traits relative to his female counterpart. This finding suggests that partisan stereotypes overwhelm stereotypes about gender for both female and male Republican candidates. However, stereotypes about women significantly affected the probability of listing a *negative* masculine trait about a Republican female candidate. This result partially supports the trait-attribution prediction and offers evidence that gender can constrain the influence of masculine partisan stereotypes. Respondents may see traits such as being strong, tough, and decisive as undesirable qualities for Republican women but not for Republican men.

The analyses offer partial support for the trait-attribution and -application hypotheses. Respondents were equally likely to attribute Democratic female and male candidates with partisan traits—suggesting that voters do not use either a reinforcing or an additive model to form trait

SYLVIA I. GONZALEZ AND NICHOLE M. BAUER

impressions of Democratic candidates but rely on partisan stereotypes. We build on these results with an experiment that directly manipulates the salience of candidate sex and party while controlling the partisan trait information participants have about each candidate This experiment tests how voters respond to candidates who make strategic appeals using partisan traits.

EMPIRICAL TEST 2: AN EXPERIMENT TEST OF TRAIT APPLICATION

The second empirical test, a national survey experiment, tracks how voters respond to candidates who directly emphasize partisan traits in a test of the trait-application prediction. A key difference between the experiment and the ANES analyses is that, rather than asking participants to generate trait content about specific candidates, we asked participants to respond to candidates who emphasized partisan traits. The trait-application prediction argues that participants will respond negatively to female candidates who emphasize gendered traits, even if these qualities map onto partisan stereotypes. The high level of control over the information presented to participants in an experimental context ensures that voters have the *same* type of information about candidates and that the information reflects partisan-trait content. The experiment uses a 2×2×2 factorial design, manipulating candidate sex (male or female), partisanship (Democratic or Republican), and the traits attributed to the candidates (partisan or none). We do not manipulate race in this experiment as we are attempting to isolate the causal mechanisms at work in voter perceptions across the sexes, and including a race treatment can inadvertently alter subject responses.

The experimental sample comes from the 2014 Cooperative Congressional Election Study (CCES). The CCES consists of two waves during election years and uses a stratified sampling method to generate samples that approximately matches the US population on critical characteristics (Vavreck and Rivers 2008). The names Karen Bailey and Kevin Bailey, along with photos, cued candidate sex. The partisan-trait condition for Democrats described the candidate as *caring* and *sensitive,* and the partisan-trait condition for Republicans described the candidate as *tough* and *assertive.* We use these traits because they align with partisan traits (Hayes 2005; Winter 2010), and with broader traits related to gender stereotypes (Eagly and Karau 2002). The control conditions removed the traits. We embedded these manipulations in a screenshot of the candidate's home

Table 5.1. The Effects of Candidate Sex on Trait Attribution

| | DEMOCRATIC CANDIDATES | | | | REPUBLICAN CANDIDATES | | | |
| | Feminine Traits | | Masculine Traits | | Feminine Traits | | Masculine Traits | |
	Positive	Negative	Positive	Negative	Positive	Negative	Positive	Negative
Female Candidate	-0.058 (0.098)	-0.128 (0.171)	0.157 (0.112)	0.069 (0.227)	-0.264** (0.134)	-0.313 (0.377)	0.083 (0.131)	0.571* (0.340)
Incumbent Candidate	0.348*** (0.089)	-0.017 (0.172)	0.228** (0.107)	0.367 (0.233)	0.032 (0.089)	-0.034 (0.171)	0.110 (0.092)	-0.127 (0.289)
Democrat Respondent	0.087 (0.131)	0.266 (0.379)	0.145 (0.144)	0.029 (0.394)	-0.011 (0.131)	0.194 (0.310)	-0.002 (0.142)	3.429*** (0.333)
Republican Respondent	-0.038 (0.134)	0.669* (0.385)	-0.014 (0.153)	0.161 (0.407)	-0.213* (0.122)	0.268 (0.360)	0.010 (0.135)	3.474*** (0.300)
Female Respondent	0.206*** (0.063)	-0.267* (0.162)	-0.193** (0.076)	-0.616*** (0.233)	0.208** (0.087)	-0.432** (0.196)	-0.070 (0.074)	-0.656** (0.296)
Political Knowledge	0.117 (0.102)	0.303 (0.242)	0.420*** (0.122)	0.491 (0.334)	-0.123 (0.133)	0.145 (0.283)	0.257** (0.124)	-0.542 (0.495)

Election Year	-0.055^{***} (0.017)	0.054^{**} (0.022)	0.091^{***} (0.017)	0.027 (0.027)	-0.025 (0.017)	-0.005 (0.024)	0.044^{***} (0.015)	0.029 (0.049)
Constant	108.7^{***} (34.38)	-109.4^{**} (44.37)	-183.1^{***} (32.85)	-56.95 (53.43)	49.05 (34.73)	8.550 (48.91)	-88.69^{***} (29.96)	-62.40 (97.91)
N	1956	1525	1956	1525	1803	1332	1803	1332
adj. R^2	0.0306	0.0613	0.0527	0.0902	0.0176	0.0344	0.0135	0.1077

Note: Robust standard errors in parentheses, $^* p < 0.10$, $^{**} p < 0.05$, $^{***} p < 0.01$

page on their campaign website. Using a website for the manipulation reflects the way many individuals learn about candidates outside the experimental lab as most candidates for political office use websites to promote their campaigns (Druckman, Kifer, and Parkin 2009).

We include three outcome variables. First, participants rated candidate *experience*. We include this variable because female candidates often receive negative ratings on experience (Schneider and Bos 2014). Next, each participant rated how well the phrase *good representative of constituent opinion* described the candidate. This question assesses the viability and quality of a candidate (Brooks 2013; Elis, Hillygus, and Nie 2010). Participants also rated how qualified they thought the candidate was to move onto *higher levels of political office*. These measures are alternatives to a vote-choice question. Asking directly about vote choice may not be effective in an experimental design because this study only presents participants with one candidate (Bauer 2015a, Brooks 2013). Additionally, support for female candidates may decrease as the level of office at stake increases (Huddy and Terkildsen 1993; Rosenwasser and Seale 1988), and the higher-office question can capture this effect. We rescaled each variable to range from 0 to 1 with higher values indicating evaluations that are more positive.

Based on the trait-application hypothesis, we predict that partisan-trait appeals will benefit Democratic female candidates but not Republican female candidates. We use a series of two-tailed t-tests (figure 5.1). First, we compare the candidate evaluations from the partisan-trait condition to the control condition for each candidate. For example, we compare the Republican female candidate's rating in the partisan condition to her rating in the control condition. Comparisons from the treatment to the control condition are necessary because voters do not always extend the stereotypes about the parties to individual candidates (Goggin and Theodoridis 2016). The final comparison uses a difference-in-differences (DID) approach to compare the difference in evaluations from the partisan conditions to the control condition within candidate partisanship but across candidate sex. If gender stereotypes affect responses to trait strategies in line with the trait-application prediction, then the female candidate should receive less positive evaluations compared to her co-partisan male counterpart.[2]

The Democratic female candidate's evaluations do not change from the partisan-trait condition to the control condition on the experience and good-representative ratings. Emphasizing partisan traits shifts the Dem-

SYLVIA I. GONZALEZ AND NICHOLE M. BAUER

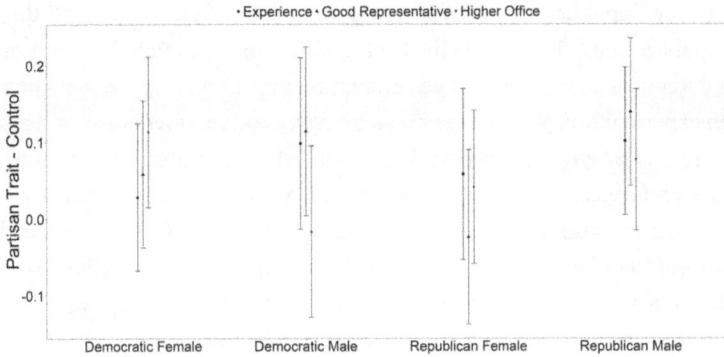

· Experience · Good Representative · Higher Office

Figure 5.1. The Effects of Emphasizing Partisan Traits on Candidate Evaluations
Note: 95% confidence intervals included.

ocratic female candidate's evaluation on the higher-office question where there is a 0.113, or a boost of 11.3%, $p = 0.0260$. This positive effect runs counter to the trait-application prediction but does offer support for the joint influence of partisan and gender stereotypes on how voters responded to the feminine trait messages of Democratic female candidates. All the candidates were running for a Senate seat, a fairly high level of office, and the assumption is that the higher level of office primes participants to think about the candidate serving as president—making this result more striking.

The Democratic male candidate receives a marginally significant 9.8% boost on experience, $p = 0.0880$, and a boost of 11.4% on being a good representative of constituent opinion, $p = 0.0421$, but the evaluation does not significantly change on the higher-office measure, $p = 0.7607$. Comparing the difference-in-differences across the two candidates shows no significant differences. While the Democratic male candidate benefits more with partisan traits in the treatment condition relative to the control condition, he does not necessarily benefit more compared to the Democratic female candidate across those same two conditions. These effects could indicate that, together, the results for the female and male Democratic candidates provide partial support for the trait-application prediction. Explicitly emphasizing feminine partisan traits can, under some conditions, benefit Democratic female candidates, but feminine traits will lead to more consistently positive effects for Democratic male candidates.

The Republican male candidate gains a significant boost on all three variables, and this supports the trait-application prediction. For example, the Republican male candidate's evaluation improves by 10.1%, $p = 0.0053$, on experience, 13.9%, $p = 0.0053$, on being a good representative, and 7.7% increase on being qualified for higher office that just falls short of statistical significance, $p = 0.1042$ ($p = 0.0521$ with a one-tailed test). Emphasizing partisan masculine traits enhances the qualifications of Republican male but not Republican female candidates. The positive boost received by the Republican male candidate offers support for a partisan model where voters see masculine traits as a strength. The lack of any significant effect of masculine traits for the Republican female candidate offers support for a gender-stereotyping model where voters do not see these traits as desirable or helpful qualities for Republican women.

Discussion

We offer several critical conclusions about the relationship between gender and partisan stereotypes in evaluations of female political candidates. First, the results show that, even if voters attribute partisan traits to female candidates, this does not necessarily mean that voters will see these traits as a benefit to all female candidates. Emphasizing masculine traits, even though they are partisan-consistent qualities, does little to move the impressions voters form of Republican female candidates. Second, the relationship between gender and partisan stereotypes is not static, but there are times when gender and partisan stereotypes have an interactive relationship when voters attribute traits to female candidates. This interactive relationship can shift, however, so that gender stereotypes dominate partisan stereotypes when voters respond to candidate-trait strategies. Third, the relationship between gender and partisan stereotypes changes across candidate party and candidate sex. The way voters consider gender and partisan stereotypes in evaluations of a Republican female candidate is not the same relationship for a Republican male candidate. These results offer a theoretical framework applicable to the intersectional identities of political candidates beyond just the relationship between party and gender stereotypes but stereotypes about race, religion, or social class status, among other identities.

An underlying assumption of the gender, partisan, and interactive models is that these models of stereotyping in politics are mutually exclusive. For example, the partisan approach assumes that voters will always use partisan stereotypes to ascribe traits to political candidates (Dolan 2014). Even if voters ascribe the same traits to female and male candidates, however, they do not always use those traits to make the same types of decisions about female and male candidates. For instance, if a voter sees a Democratic woman and a Democratic man as empathetic, this suggests the use of a partisan model and that gender has no bearing on evaluations. Voters may see empathy as a strength in a Democratic man and a weakness in a Democratic female candidate, and this suggests the influence of gender stereotypes. These findings have critical implications for delineating the role of gender bias in voter decision-making, candidate strategies, and how voters evaluate candidates who fit into multiple stereotyped groups.

Scholars, pundits, and campaign strategists debate which messages and strategies will produce the most positive outcomes for women pursuing political office. A common approach to detecting such bias is through comparisons of the traits voters attribute to female relative to male candidates. Some scholars argue that female candidates benefit from the same strategies as male candidates, thereby implying that gender stereotypes do not factor into voter decision-making (Hayes and Lawless 2016). This research shows that voters seeing female and male candidates as having the same traits does not mean that voters will use those traits to form the same positive impressions of female and male candidates. Indeed, voters frequently see female candidates who have feminine traits as unviable political contenders for political office (Bauer 2015a; Ditonto, Hamilton, and Redlawsk 2014) while at the same time evaluating female candidates with masculine traits as unlikable (Bauer and Carpinella 2018). A strategy that plays on partisan stereotypes may work for a male candidate but will not necessarily produce the same result when the candidate is a woman.

We have found two broader patterns in women's representation. First, Democratic women fare better than Republican women in electoral politics. Indeed, most women who run for political office do so as Democrats. These findings suggest that individuals have an easier time forming impressions of Democratic women because the reinforcing sex and party cues are clear and easy for individuals to process. The conflicting cues from Republican women are difficult to process, and lead individuals to see Republican women as not quite fitting the Republican Party and not fitting into the mold of being a woman. These findings fit into other research suggesting that Republican women do not fit into the party (Thomsen 2014). Future work should examine more closely whether Republican female candidates face more scrutiny because of the conflict between party and sex.

Considering only the overlap between gender and partisan stereotypes, it is difficult to include race, given its limited power in the ANES data used, which we attribute to the smaller number of women of color who ran for office in the elections during 1992 and 2000, when the data was collected. The inclusion of race in gender and politics studies is becoming increasingly important as more women of color run for office. Since there are separate stereotypes about people of color, investigating the intersection of race, sex, and partisanship is important to identifying the challenges women of color face in pursuing political office. People of color are generally perceived to be more liberal, making it necessary to consider the effect of candidate race on the relationship between gender and party. Research suggests that race and gender stereotypes can combine to provide Black and Latina women with a double advantage (Gershon and Monforti forthcoming; Cargile and Pringle forthcoming; Bejarano 2013) where it was assumed they previously had a double disadvantage. Future iterations should account for the interaction of race and sex as the ballots continue to become more diverse.

Conclusion

Personality traits are tools voters use to evaluate political candidates. Stereotypes about Democrats as compassionate and empathetic did not directly extend to Hillary Clinton. Emphasizing the right set of traits can affect voter decision-making. However, traits also tap into gender stereotypes. The relationship between gender and party may limit the ability of female candidates to emphasize a well-rounded set of personality characteristics. Female candidates may need to focus their campaign messages on masculine qualities, because these qualities are most consistent with leadership roles. Candidate sex can still pose perceptual constraints for female candidates. These constraints can reduce vote support for female candidates, thereby contributing to the perpetual underrepresentation of women at all levels of political office in the United States.

SYLVIA I. GONZALEZ AND NICHOLE M. BAUER

Notes

1. We conducted an additional experiment to see if there were differences in the *number* of partisan traits listed about female and male Democratic and Republican candidates.

2. There were no significant differences in the control conditions.

References

Alexander, Deborah, and Kristi Anderson. 1993. "Gender as a Factor in the Attribution of Leadership Traits." *Political Research Quarterly* 46 (3): 527–45.

Barnes, Tiffany D., and Emily Beaulieu. 2014. "Gender Stereotypes and Corruption: How Candidates Affect Perceptions of Election Fraud." *Politics & Gender* 10: 365–91.

Bauer, Nichole M. 2015a. "Emotional, Sensitive, and Unfit for Office: Gender Stereotype Activation and Support for Female Candidates." *Political Psychology* 36 (6): 691–708.

———. 2015b. "Who Stereotypes Female Candidates? Identifying Individual Differences in Feminine Stereotype Reliance." *Politics, Groups, and Identities* 3 (1): 94–110.

———. 2018. "Untangling the Relationship between Partisanship, Gender Stereotypes, and Support for Female Candidates." *Journal of Women, Politics & Policy* 39 (1).

———. 2019a. "The Effects of Partisan Trespassing Strategies across Candidate Sex." *Political Behavior* 41 (4): 897–915.

———. 2019b. "A Feminine Advantage? Delineating the Effects of Feminine Trait and Feminine Issues Messages on Evaluations of Female Candidates." *Politics & Gender.* Forthcoming.

Bauer, Nichole M., and Colleen Carpinella. 2018. "Visual Communication and Candidate Evaluation: The Influence of Feminine and Masculine Images on Support for Female Candidates." *Political Research Quarterly* 71 (2): 395–407.

Bejarano, Christina. 2013. *The Latina Advantage: Gender, Race, and Political Success.* Austin: University of Texas Press.

Biernat, Monica, Melvin Manis, and Thomas E. Nelson. 1991. "Stereotypes and Standards of Judgment." *Journal of Personality and Social Psychology* 60 (4): 485–99.

Bos, Angela L., Monica C. Schneider, and Brittany L. Utz. 2017. "Gender Stereotypes and Prejudice in U.S. Elections." In *APA Handbook of the Psychology of Women,* ed. Cheryl Travis and Jackie White, 367–84. Washington, DC: American Psychological Association.

Bracic, Ana, Mackenzie Israel-Trummel, and Allyson Shortle. 2019. "Is Sexism for White People? Gender Stereotypes, Race, and the 2016 Presidential Election." *Political Behavior* 41 (2): 281–307.

Brooks, Deborah Jordan. 2013. *He Runs, She Runs*. Princeton, NJ: Princeton University Press.

Cargile, Ivy A. M., and Lisa Pringle. Forthcoming. "Context not Candidate Sex: A Case study of Female Vote Choice for Mayor." *Urban Affairs Review*.

Cassese, Erin C., and Mirya R. Holman. 2018. "Party and Gender Stereotypes in Campaign Attacks." *Political Behavior* 40 (3): 785–807.

———. 2019. "Playing the Woman Card: Ambivalent Sexism in the 2016 U.S. Presidential Race." *Political Psychology* 40 (1): 55–74.

Conroy, Meredith. 2015. *Masculinity, Media, and the American Presidency*. New York: Palgrave McMillan.

Ditonto, Tessa M. 2017. "A High Bar or a Double Standard? Gender, Competence, and Information in Political Campaigns." *Political Behavior* 39 (2): 301–25.

Ditonto, Tessa M., Allison J. Hamilton, and David P. Redlawsk. 2014. "Gender Stereotypes, Information Search, and Voting Behavior in Political Campaigns." *Political Behavior* 36 (2): 335–58.

Dolan, Kathleen. 2014. *When Does Gender Matter? Women Candidates & Gender Stereotypes in American Elections*. New York: Oxford University Press.

Druckman, James N., Martin J. Kifer, and Michael Parkin. 2009. "Campaign Communications in U.S. Congressional Elections." *American Political Science Review* 103 (3): 343–66.

Eagly, Alice H., and Steve J. Karau. 2002. "Role Congruity Theory of Prejudice Toward Female Leaders." *Psychological Review* 109 (3): 573–94.

Elis, Roy, D. Sunshine Hillygus, and Norman Nie. 2010. "The Dynamics of Candidate Evaluations and Vote Choice in 2008: Looking to the Past or Future?" *Electoral Studies* 29 (4): 582–93.

Gershon, Sarah Allen, and Jessica Lavariega Monforti. Forthcoming. "Intersecting Campaigns: Candidate Race, Ethnicity, Gender and Voter Evaluations." *Politics, Groups, and Identities*.

Goggin, Stephen N., and Alexander G. Theodoridis. 2016. "Disputed Ownership: Parties, Issues, and Traits in the Minds of Voters." *Political Behavior* 39 (3): 675–702.

Hayes, Danny. 2005. "Candidate Qualities through a Partisan Lens: A Theory of Trait Ownership." *American Journal of Political Science* 49 (4): 908–23.

———. 2011. "When Gender and Party Collide: Stereotyping in Candidate Trait Attribution." *Politics & Gender* 7 (2): 133–65.

Hayes, Danny, and Jennifer L. Lawless. 2016. *Women on the Run: Gender, Media, and Political Campaigns in a Polarized Era*. New York: Cambridge University Press.

Holman, Mirya R., Jennifer L. Merolla, and Elizabeth J. Zechmeister. 2016. "Terrorist Threat, Male Stereotypes, and Candidate Evaluations." *Political Research Quarterly* 69 (1): 134–47.

Huddy, Leonie, and Nayda Terkildsen. 1993. "Gender Stereotypes and the Perception of Male and Female Candidates." *American Journal of Political Science* 37 (1): 119–47.

Koch, Jeffrey W. 2001. "When Parties and Candidates Collide: Citizen Perception of House Candidates' Positions on Abortion." *Public Opinion Quarterly* 65: 1–21.

Krupnikov, Yanna, and Nichole M. Bauer. 2014. "The Relationship Between Campaign Negativity, Gender and Campaign Context." *Political Behavior* 36 (1): 167–88.

Kunda, Ziva, and Paul Thagard. 1996. "Forming Impressions from Stereotypes, Traits, and Behaviors: A Parallel-Constraint-Satisfaction Theory." *Psychological Review* 103 (2): 284–308.

Mason, Lilliana, and Julie Wronski. 2018. "One Tribe to Bind Them All: How Our Social Group Attachments Strengthen Partisanship." *Advances in Political Psychology* 39 (1): 257–78.

Petrocik, John R. 1996. "Issue Ownership in Presidential Elections, with a 1980 Case Study." *American Journal of Political Science* 40 (3): 825–50.

Rahn, Wendy M. 1993. "The Role of Partisan Stereotypes in Information Processing about Political Candidates." *American Journal of Political Science* 37 (2): 472–96.

Riker, William. 1996. *The Strategy of Rhetoric: Campaigning for the American Constitution.* New Haven, CT: Yale University Press.

Rosenwasser, Shirley Miller, and Jana Seale. 1988. "Attitudes Toward a Hypothetical Male or Female Presidential Candidate—A Research Note." *Political Psychology* 9 (4): 591–98.

Sanbonmatsu, Kira, and Kathleen Dolan. 2009. "Do Gender Stereotypes Transcend Party?" *Political Research Quarterly* 62 (3): 485–94.

Schneider, Monica C., and Angela L. Bos. 2014. "Measuring Stereotypes of Female Politicians." *Political Psychology* 35 (2): 245–66.

———. 2016. "The Intersection of Party and Gender Stereotypes in Evaluating Political Candidates." *Journal of Women, Politics & Policy* 37 (3): 274–94.

Sides, John. 2006. "The Origins of Campaign Agendas." *British Journal of Political Science* 36 (3): 407–36.

Simon, Adam F. 2002. *The Winning Message: Candidate Behavior, Campaign Discourse, and Democracy.* New York: Cambridge University Press.

Sulkin, Tracy, and Nathaniel Swigger. 2008. "Is There Truth in Advertising? Campaign Ad Images as Signals about Legislative Behavior." *Journal of Politics* 70 (1): 232–44.

Thomsen, Danielle. 2014. "Ideological Moderates Won't Run: How Party Fit Matters for Partisan Polarization in Congress." *Journal of Politics* 76 (3): 786–97.

Valentino, Nicholas A., Carly Wayne, and Marzia Oceno. 2018. "Mobilizing Sexism: The Interaction of Emotion and Gender Attitudes in the 2016 US Presidential Election." *Public Opinion Quarterly* 82 (Special Issue 2018): 213–35.

Vavreck, Lynn, and Douglas Rivers. 2008. "The 2006 Cooperative Congressional Election Study." *Journal of Elections, Public Opinion and Parties* 18 (4): 355–66.

Winter, Nicholas J. G. 2010. "Masculine Republicans and Feminine Democrats: Gender and Americans' Explicit and Implicit Images of the Political Parties." *Political Behavior* 32 (4): 587–618.

SYLVIA I. GONZALEZ AND NICHOLE M. BAUER

BEYOND THE PRESIDENCY, 2016

Women Candidates in Concurrent Down-Ballot Races

TESSA DITONTO AND DAVID J. ANDERSEN

illary Clinton's 2016 candidacy for the presidency was an important moment for women's political representation in the United States. Much has been written about the experiences of Clinton herself and about the significance of a woman running as a major-party presidential nominee for the first time. However, far less attention has been paid to the experiences of the other women who ran for office across the country in the same year. Twenty sixteen saw more women running for office than any other previous year, which suggests significant strides for women's representation. On the other hand, 2016 was one of the few election cycles since 1992 in which women gained no seats in Congress. Similarly, experimental research has found that down-ballot women may be disadvantaged when other women run for higher office simultaneously, as gender-based stereotypes and biases become more salient to voters when they are asked to consider supporting multiple women at once (Ditonto and Andersen 2018). In 2016, for the first time in the United States, every voter in the country saw a woman at the top of their ticket. While an important milestone in and of itself, it is also possible that this served to disadvantage women running down-ballot.

While Ditonto and Andersen (2018) suggest that Clinton's candidacy may have served as an obstacle to other women's electoral success, this hypothesis has only been tested in an experimental setting. Of course, experimental research is limited, since it trades elements of real-world generalizability for the ability to draw causal inferences. Finding experimental evidence that the presence of multiple women on the ballot can serve as an obstacle to individual female candidates does not necessarily mean that those findings will translate to actual elections with all of their complexity.

Will such a pattern of experimental findings emerge in a real election? Since Democrats saw the first female presidential candidate from a major party at the top of their ticket, 2016 provides an excellent opportunity to find out. We utilize data from the 2016 Cooperative Congressional Election Study in order to examine whether the number of other women running for office simultaneously affected voters' willingness to support female House candidates. We find that, even in actual elections, female candidates in down-ballot races may be less likely to win when they run at the same time as other women further up the ballot. Democrats, in particular, follow the same general pattern as subjects in our experiments. When the only other in-party female candidate they saw was Hillary Clinton, Democrats were actually more likely to support a female in-party House candidate than a male in-party House candidate. However, when they saw another woman running for either Senate or governor, they became far less likely to support their female House candidate. Republicans, on the other hand, were less likely to support female candidates who ran in isolation, but were *more* likely to support female House candidates when other women also appeared on the ballot.

Candidate Sex and Voter Decision-Making

The underrepresentation of women in elected office in the United States is undeniable.[1] Political science research points to multiple causes for this phenomenon, including differences in the candidate-emergence process (Lawless and Fox 2005) and various structural barriers to women's success (Palmer and Simon 2008; Sanbonmatsu 2006). On the other hand, the role of voter bias and stereotypes is unclear. Findings from aggregate vote totals (looking at one election at a time) have found that women are no less likely to win their races than men are (Burrell 1994; Seltzer, Newman, and Leighton 1997; Darcy, Welch, and Clark 1994; Woods 2000; Dolan 2004). On the other hand, evidence suggests that voters may hold a number of gender-based stereotypes that they apply to female candidates, including that they are more feminine, communal, emotional, warm, and gentle, but that they are less masculine, agentic, assertive, competent, and strong (Huddy and Terkildsen 1993a; Kahn 1996; Leeper 1991; Alexander and Andersen 1993; Cook, Thomas, and Wilcox 1994; Dolan 2004; Rosenwasser and Seale 1988).

TESSA DITONTO AND DAVID J. ANDERSEN

While some scholars have found that these stereotypes may not affect election outcomes (Dolan 2014; Brooks 2013; Hayes 2011), others have found that their influence may be contingent upon multiple aspects of the overall electoral environment, such as whether feminine or masculine issues are salient (Cook, Thomas, and Wilcox 1994; Dolan 2004; Holman, Merolla, and Zechmeister 2011; Lawless 2004), which office is being sought (Huddy and Terkildsen 1993b; Ono and Burden 2019), whether feminine stereotypes are activated by campaign messages (Bauer 2015a), and which voters one looks at (Bauer 2015b). Further, evidence suggests that women in leadership roles are subject to stereotypes and biases that women in general may not be. Specifically, assumptions that women are higher in communal traits like compassion, sensitivity, and nurturing are seen as incongruent with expectations that leaders are agentic, strong, and assertive (Eagly 1987; Eagly and Karau 2002). Schneider and Bos (2013) similarly find that female candidates are perceived as a subtype of women and subject to unique stereotypes related to masculine and leadership characteristics. Finally, Ditonto, Hamilton, and Redlawsk (2014), and Ditonto (2017; 2018) find that female candidates are evaluated more heavily on the "masculine" trait of competence than male candidates and that this can pose problems for them if they are portrayed as lacking in competence.

Importantly, almost all of this literature considers female candidates running only in single races, as if each election were contested in isolation. The United States' electoral system requires voters to learn about and evaluate candidates for multiple races simultaneously, however, and this may have implications for individual candidates. While it is obvious that a candidate running for a seat in Congress will be judged in relation to their opponent for the same seat, for example, it is also likely that voters' evaluations of that candidate will be influenced by the candidates running for Senate, governor, or president at the same time as well. To better understand candidate evaluation in the American context, then, it may be helpful to consider who is running in other concurrent races, too.

Female Candidates and Concurrent Elections

For this reason, we posit that, if we want to understand how voters' attitudes and behavior affect individual female candidates, then we should examine the gender composition of all of the races being contested simultaneously in one election cycle. The number of campaigns being waged at the same time will drastically alter the information environment in which a vote decision must be made. The more offices on the ballot, the more total information a voter must gather in order to make an informed set of vote decisions. Though Americans are a notoriously politically uninformed and inattentive population, in general (Delli Carpini and Keeter 1996), political psychologists have demonstrated that voters are often able to use information shortcuts as a means of making relatively high-quality decisions without having to gather all relevant information (Lau and Redlawsk 1997; Lupia and McCubbins 2000). Presumably, as a campaign environment becomes more crowded, these heuristics become more and more useful, because voters learn less information about each set of candidates and must rely upon shortcuts (Wolak 2009, Andersen 2010).

If choosing a senator, for example, were our only life task, we would certainly have the time and energy necessary to learn all there was to know about the candidates for that office. In reality however, the United States is unique in the sheer number of elections that are often contested at the same time. Americans typically have multiple high-level offices to learn about in any given campaign season, and these tasks are on top of other state and local races as well, not to mention more pertinent concerns like family and work.

The total number of women running in all of these races is consequential for female candidates, thanks to a combination of the negative content of many gender stereotypes and the still-novel context of seeing multiple women on the same ballot. Even if voters still harbor doubts about women as political leaders, other politically relevant information (like partisanship) may override those doubts in individual races, especially races in which the candidates are well-known. However, the negative content of many gender-based stereotypes—specifically the underlying assumption that feminine gender roles and leadership roles are incongruent, and that women are less qualified, strong, and competent (Eagly and Karau 2002; Schneider and Bos 2013)—means that they may disadvantage female candidates if and when they are applied by voters. Election cycles that include women running for multiple offices simultaneously may "activate" gender stereotypes for voters (Sinclair and Kunda 1999; Kunda and Spencer 2003; Bauer 2015a) in ways that seeing one woman in a field otherwise comprised of men may not.

TESSA DITONTO AND DAVID J. ANDERSEN

Though more women are running for office with each election cycle, the reality of American elections is that most candidates are still men, so voters likely still expect (either consciously or unconsciously) to see mainly men on their ballots. The presence of multiple women in one election cycle may draw voters' attention to gender in a number of ways. First, the sheer novelty of many women running at once may be enough to trigger gender-based stereotypes and/or prejudices in voters. Second, as more women run at the same time, gender and gendered policy issues may become more salient in that election cycle, with the media and candidates themselves spending more time addressing these things in their communication with the public. As gender becomes more relevant in an election cycle, gender-based stereotypes may become more accessible and, therefore, a more readily used heuristic by voters.

Additionally, we also expect that gender may matter more for the candidates that voters know the least about. Gender cues serve as proxies for other information. Because stereotypic information is more salient when less individuating information is incorporated into a person's judgment (Locksley et al. 1980; Locksley, Hepburn, and Ortiz 1982; Ashmore 1981; Eagly and Wood 1982), our best chance to observe the effect of such cues may be in offices where voters are least likely to learn much specific information about the candidates (and thus are less likely to counteract stereotypes/prejudices). Assuming that voters have a fixed amount of time and energy that they are able and willing to devote to an election, as the number of offices on the ballot increases, voters can either learn an equal amount of information about the candidates for each office—thereby decreasing the amount they learn about each candidate equally—or they can slim their information demands by learning relatively less about some offices and more about others. Either way, candidates in offices that receive less attention are likely subject to stereotypes and other heuristics to a greater extent than candidates in races to which voters devote a lot of time and attention. If heuristics become more important to voters as their information environments become more crowded, then, voters should rely more heavily on cues like a candidate's sex as more offices are added to the ballot.

Congressional candidates have the lowest average campaign spending and lowest recognition among the major offices, and voters tend to spend less effort and attention in learning about congressional than higher-office candidates. Therefore, it may be that the effects of multiple concurrent female candidates will be stronger for congressional candidates, relative to candidates for president, governor, or Senate. In fact, both Wolak (2009) and Andersen (2010) find that concurrent elections disadvantage House members, in particular, because voters tend to devote more of their attention and information search to higher offices.

Women running for Congress, then, should be more subject to gender stereotypes than women in higher offices, since voters will presumably devote less time and energy to learning about them and apply stereotypes to them more readily (though see Ono and Burden 2019 for evidence that gender stereotypes may affect women in presidential races more than lower races). When only one office is on the ballot, voters may be more willing to spend time gathering information about the candidates in the race, thereby learning enough total information to counteract gender-based or other stereotypes they may have. Similarly, when a campaign environment is crowded and a higher-level office like the presidency is contested alongside a House race, voters may take the time to learn about the presidential candidates while relying on stereotypes, like those based on gender, to a greater degree when it comes to the House.

This is precisely what we find in our 2018 experimental study.[2] Women who ran on their own did well—and even better than male candidates in some instances—but the story for women who ran alongside other women was more complicated. This was especially true for women who ran for lower office while another woman also sought election to an office further up the ballot. Female House candidates were both liked less and received participants' votes less often when another woman ran for higher office in the same party. What we still don't know is whether this pattern will be visible in a "real-world" election cycle, with all of its complexity and nuance.

The Role of Partisanship

Part of the complexity of real-world elections is the influence of partisanship and, of course, we expect partisanship to play an important role in this story. Because partisan cues—when they are present—are almost always the most important consideration for voters in a US election (Campbell et al. 1960; Zaller 1992; Bartels 2000; Goren, Federico, and Kittilson

TESSA DITONTO AND DAVID J. ANDERSEN

2009), we expect that partisan voters will generally only consider candidates in their own political party, or at least that it will take quite a lot to get them to consider the other party's candidate. Some evidence suggests that party cues are so important that gender stereotypes simply do not affect voter decision-making in a partisan election (Hayes 2011; Dolan 2014). There is also evidence that independents are the most likely to use gender stereotypes and/or discriminate against female candidates. This is presumably because, while partisans are often willing to vote for their own party's candidate regardless of that candidate's individual characteristics, independents rely on other considerations. This may leave more "space" for gender-based stereotypes and biases to have an effect (Ono and Burden 2019; Andersen and Ditonto forthcoming).

Candidate sex and partisanship have been shown to interact in other ways, as well. For example, there is evidence that women who run as Republicans are evaluated less favorably by their own partisans than women who run as Democrats (Bauer 2015a; Sanbonmatsu and Dolan 2009; King and Matland 2003), and women are more likely to run and be successful in Democratic than Republican primaries, as well (Gaddie and Bullock 1995; Palmer and Simon 2008; Lawless and Pearson 2008). Finally, candidates who seek to counter gender-based stereotypes may be successful with co-partisans but face backlash from out-party subjects (Krupnikov and Bauer 2014; Bauer 2017).

Taken together, this evidence suggests that the partisanship of voters as well as candidates will have an effect on the fates of individual female candidates, as well. For this reason, we look separately at whether voters see women running in their own political party or in the opposing party, and we control for voters' strength of partisanship. We expect that candidate sex will matter differently depending upon whether women are running in a voter's preferred party (their "in-party" or their non-preferred "out-party"), and that Republicans and Democrats may also react differently to seeing multiple women on their ballot. We discuss our specific hypotheses below, but evidence suggests that seeing women in one's in-party will make voters more likely to consider voting for out-party (male) candidates, while seeing women in one's out-party should make voters even more likely to vote for their in-party candidates. Further, we expect that Republican women be particularly disadvantaged, in general.

Hypotheses

We expect to see that the number of women running concurrently in different elections will affect the electoral fates of those women. We believe that most Americans care predominantly about political party and other politically relevant characteristics when evaluating candidates, and that the effects of gender may or may not be visible in any single race considered in isolation. However, as more women run for office at the same time, we expect that gender cues will begin to have a larger effect on evaluations of women candidates, and that the effects of gender will become more pronounced. Thus:

> H1: When one female candidate runs within a voter's preferred party, and no other female candidates appear on the ballot, any negative effects of gender should be small or nonexistent, mirroring findings from other recent studies that political party cues will drown out concerns about gender.

> H2: When a female candidate runs within a voter's preferred party, and other in-party women appear elsewhere on the ballot, she will be evaluated more negatively and will have a lower likelihood of obtaining a subject's vote. The greater the number of in-party women appearing in other races, the worse she will do.

These hypotheses will apply to Democrats and Republicans slightly differently in 2016, since all Democrats saw a female in-party candidate at the top of their ticket, while Republicans did not. As stated in H1, we expect that female House candidates will do worse as more women appear elsewhere on the ballot, which means that Republicans who only see a female House candidate in their party should be just as likely to vote for her as those who see male House candidates. However, if they see a Republican woman running for either Senate or governor, they should be less likely to support their female House candidate.

The 2016 Democratic ballot adds some complexity to our hypotheses, since every Democrat saw a woman in the presidential race. It is impossible to know whether Democratic female House candidates would have done better without Hillary Clinton at the top of the ticket, so all we can do is determine whether they do worse when other women, over and above Clinton, appear on the ballot. Therefore, we adjust our hypothesis such that we expect Democrats who see only a female in-party House candidate and Hillary Clinton should be more likely to support their female House candidate than those who also see a woman running for Senate or governor in their own party.

Method

To test our hypotheses, we used data from the 2016 Cooperative Congressional Election Study (CCES),[3] which is a large, nationally representative, two-wave survey (pre- and post-election), stratified by state and type of district. The 2016 study included 64,600 respondents, with state level subsamples ranging from 99 (in Wyoming) to 6,021 (in California). The survey was conducted via YouGov in October and November 2016. To the CCES data, we added data on the gender composition of each race taken from the Center for American Women and Politics (CAWP).

We conduct a binomial logistic regression in which our dependent variable is whether respondents voted for their in-party House candidate. We cluster standard errors on congressional district in order to account for non-independence among respondents from the same district. Independent variables include sex of in-party House candidate, sex of out-party House candidate, and indicators as to whether any other women ran concurrently in either the in-party or the out-party. We then use interaction terms to examine vote choice for different combinations of these gender compositions. Control variables include strength of party ID, respondent sex, respondent race, respondent education, and whether there was a gubernatorial or Senate race in a respondent's state.

In 2016, respondents in 151 congressional districts saw multiple women running for office (in either party), with respondents in 69 districts seeing more than two women (again, in either party). Four districts saw multiple Republican women running simultaneously (when at least one also ran for the House), and 132 districts saw multiple Democratic women (also when at least one was running in the House). All Democrats saw Hillary Clinton at the top of the ticket, but 45 districts saw multiple Democratic women running, over and above Clinton, which means they also saw a woman run for either Senate or governor.

Results

Table 6.1 shows the results of our analysis of vote choice for in-party House candidate. Column 1 displays the results for the entire sample; column 2 looks at Republicans only, and column 3 lists results for Democrats only. Looking first at column 1, we find significant effects for many of our covariates. Looking at our variables of interest, we find that, when respondents see a female in-party House candidate but no other female candidates (except, again, that all Democrats saw Hillary Clinton at the top of the ticket), they are actually slightly more likely to vote for the in-party candidate compared to the baseline scenario of all male candidates ($b = 0.113$, significant at $p < 0.1$). However, respondents are also more likely to vote for their in-party candidate when the *out-party* candidate is female, and all others are male ($b = 0.189$, significant at $p < 0.001$).

We also find that respondents are *less* likely to vote for their in-party House candidate when the candidate is a man but other women appear simultaneously elsewhere on the ballot. Seeing the same configuration (of a male House candidate but women elsewhere) in one's out-party has no effect. Most importantly, our crucial variable of interest has the expected sign ($b = -0.153$, $p < 0.10$), suggesting that respondents are less likely to vote for a female in-party House candidate when other in-party women appear on the ballot.

Of course, combining Democrats and Republicans in the same analysis is somewhat problematic, especially in 2016, when all Democrats saw a woman at the top of their party's ticket. For that reason, we break our sample down by party and look first at results for Republicans (column 2). We see that Republicans are far less likely to vote for their in-party House candidate when she is female and the only woman on the ballot than when he is a man (and the only man; $b = -0.558$, $p < 0.001$). However, they are actually *more* likely to vote for a female in-party candidate when other women appear on the party's ticket ($b = 0.285$, $p < 0.1$). This pattern is the opposite of what we expected to find, and we can only speculate as to the reason, but we posit that it likely has to do with the nature of a district in which two Republican women would run simultaneously. It is likely that Republicans in those districts are more liberal/moderate than the average Republican district (Palmer and Simon 2006), which may make them more open to supporting a female candidate in any office.

TESSA DITONTO AND DAVID J. ANDERSEN

Table 6.1 Effects of Number of Female Candidates on Likelihood of In-Party House Vote Choice

	Variable	All Respondents (35,370)	Republicans (15,157)	Democrats (20,213)
Voter Characteristics	Constant	1.171*** (.079)	1.843*** (.123)	.594*** (.107)
	Strength of partisanship	.433*** (.022)	.438*** (.036)	.422*** (.029)
	Female	−.097** (.037)	−.265*** (.059)	.030 (.049)
	Black	.230*** (.070)	−1.529*** (.163)	.604*** (.081)
	Education	.062*** (.013)	−.059** (.020)	.158*** (.017)
Presence of Other Campaigns	Governor race	.147** (.054)	.233** (.089)	.167* (.071)
	Senate race	−.122** (.047)	.210** (.073)	−.352*** (.063)
Sex of Individual Candidates	In-party House woman; others are men	.113† (.062)	−.558*** (.065)	.480*** (.077)
	Out-party House woman; others are men	.189*** (.050)	.055 (.065)	.376*** (.085)
	In-party House man, but other in-party women	−.088* (.037)	−.715*** (.104)	.142*** (.043)
	Out-party House man, but other out-party women	.014 (.042)	−.255*** (.051)	.314*** (.091)
Multiple Women Candidates	In-party House woman + other women (any)	−.153† (.089)	.285† (.167)	−.464*** (.108)
	Pseudo−R^2	.021	.037	.038

Note: Standard errors in parentheses, † < 0.10, $^{*} p < 0.05$, $^{**} p < 0.01$, $^{***} p < 0.001$

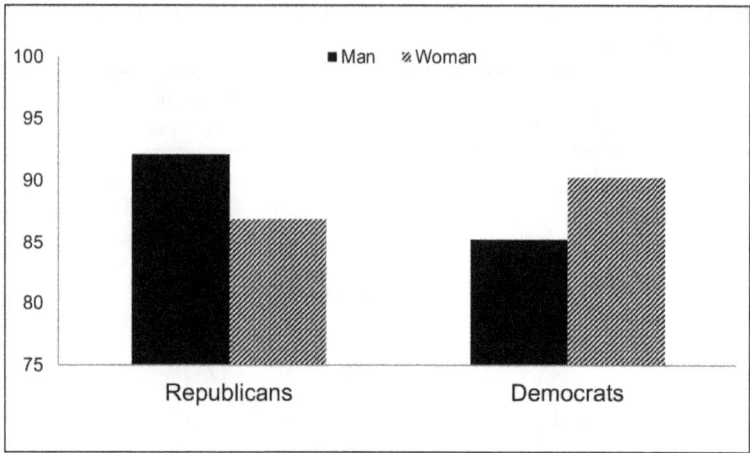

Figure 6.1. Percentage of Voting for In-Party House Candidate, based on Candidate Sex

Finally, we look at column 3 and see that it is Democrats who are driving the results that match our hypotheses, as well as our previous experimental findings. Democrats are significantly more likely to support their in-party House candidate when she is female and the only woman on the ballot other than Clinton, than when he is male (and the only man). However, when other women appear on the ballot, they are far less likely to support her (b = -0.464, p < 0.001). This suggests that our experimental evidence is holding up in the real world (among Democrats, anyway).

Beyond confirming our experimental results, this analysis also provides some interesting insights into the differences between Republicans and Democrats in willingness to support female candidates. In fact, Democrats who saw only one female candidate (over and above Hillary Clinton) were more likely to support her than a male candidate in the same scenario, but Republicans were less likely to support a lone female candidate. Figure 6.1 plots the predicted probabilities of voting for one's in-party House candidate by party and candidate sex. For Republicans, the likelihood of voting for their in-party House candidate was 92% when he was male, but only 87% when she was female. Democrats, on the other hand had an 85% chance of voting for their in-party House candidate when he was a man, but a 90% chance of doing so when she was a woman.

TESSA DITONTO AND DAVID J. ANDERSEN

Finally, while Democrats are more likely to support a woman running for Congress than a man when she is the only one running (along with Clinton), they are less likely to support a female House candidate when they also see a woman running for either Senate or governor. Democrats who saw a woman running for House along with Hillary Clinton and one other woman had an 87% chance of voting for her. Democrats who only saw a female House candidate and Clinton had a 91% chance of voting for her. It seems that Democrats may indeed have a "ceiling" on the number of women they are willing to support at once.

Discussion and Conclusion

The number of women running in concurrent elections has implications for the individual women in those races, and particularly for those running down-ballot. Specifically, Democratic women running for Congress seem to be disadvantaged as more women simultaneously run for higher office. We expect that the effects seen here would not be limited to Congress, but may well continue even further down the ballot, serving as a barrier to women running for all types of lower offices. A future test of this broader hypothesis would involve analyzing state legislative races, or other statewide executive offices.

The story for Republicans is quite different, however. While Democratic female House candidates actually do better than male candidates when they are the only woman on the ballot (aside from Hillary Clinton), Republican female House candidates do *worst* when they are the only woman on the Republican ballot. Further, while Democratic female House candidates do worse when another woman runs for a higher office, Republican female House candidates actually do *better* when other women appear on the ballot. This was a completely unexpected finding and the opposite of what we see for Democrats in this analysis or the subjects in our experimental study. We can only speculate as to why this might be the case, but it is possible that it has something to do with the nature of the districts in which multiple women run as Republicans. These are likely more moderate districts, and though our analysis is at the individual level and controls for strength of partisanship, there may be district-level differences that lead to this trend. Additionally, there are far fewer districts in which Republican voters saw multiple women than Democratic districts where voters saw multiple women, so the positive coefficient for Republicans could be driven entirely by the nuances of a very small number candidacies. (See Cooperman's essay in this volume for more on the challenges facing Republican women.) This peculiar finding requires further research.

In general, given that 2016 gave us our first presidential major-party run for a female candidate and that 2018 was another record-breaking year for women's candidacies, these findings are potentially troubling for female candidates. While both the 2016 and the 2018 election cycles resulted in significant progress for women's representation in American politics, our findings suggest that such an increase in women's candidacies may not always have a universally positive effect on other female candidates. As we see more and more women running—particularly for higher offices—our findings suggest that lower-office female candidates may be negatively affected at the ballot box. That this is especially true for Democrats is also problematic, since most women who run do so as Democrats.

The story, though, is not entirely negative, and is not as consistently negative as the findings from our experimental study. Our results do suggest that Democratic women who appear on the ballot with only one other woman (at the very top of the ticket, no less) actually have an advantage over their male counterparts. Further respondents who live in Republican districts in which multiple women run also tend to support female candidates. Women are running and receiving support in both parties, even in the presence of other female candidates. Clearly, the dynamics that determine when the presence of multiple women is a help or a hindrance to individual female candidates are nuanced and deserve further examination.

Notes

1. See the Center for American Women in Politics for the latest numbers: www.cawp.rutgers.edu.

2. Hennings and Urbatsch (2015) find a similar result in which women at the top of a ticket are much more likely to have a running mate of the opposite sex than men are.

3. Stephen Ansolabehere and Brian F. Schaffner, "Cooperative Congressional Election Study, 2016: Common Content," August 4, 2017 (Cambridge, MA: Harvard University), cces.gov.harvard.edu.

References

Alexander, Deborah, and Kristi Andersen. 1993. "Gender as a Factor in the Attribution of Leadership Traits." *Political Research Quarterly* 46 (3): 527–45.

Andersen, David J. 2010. "The Down-Ballot Problem: Concurrent Elections and Cognitive Limitations on Voting Behavior." American Political Science Association Annual Meeting, Washington, DC.

Andersen, David J., and Tessa Ditonto. 2020. "The Importance of Candidate Sex and Partisan Preference Over Time: A Multi-day Study of Voter Decision-Making." *Journal of Politics,* forthcoming.

Ashmore, R. D. 1981. "Sex Stereotypes and Implicit Personality Theory." In *Cognitive Processes in Stereotyping and Intergroup Behavior,* ed. E. L. Hamildon. Hilldale, NJ: Erlbaum.

Bauer, Nichole M. 2015a. "Emotional, Sensitive, and Unfit for Office: Stereotype Activation and Support for Female Candidates." *Political Psychology* 36 (6): 691–708.

———. 2015b. "Who Stereotypes Female Candidates." *Politics, Groups, & Identities* 3 (1): 94–110.

———. 2017. "The Effects of Counterstereotypic Gender Strategies on Candidate Evaluations." *Political Psychology* 38 (2): 279–95.

Berinsky, Adam. 2002. "Political Context and the Survey Response: The Dynamics of Racial Policy Opinion." *Journal of Politics* 64 (2): 567–84.

Berinsky, Adam, Gregory A. Huber, and Gabriel S. Lenz. 2012. "Evaluating Online Labor Markets for Experimental Research: Amazon.com's Mechanical Turk." *Political Analysis* 20 (3): 351–88.

Berinsky, Adam, and Howard Lavine. 2007. "Self-Monitoring and Political Attitudes." In *Improving Public Opinion Surveys,* ed. John Aldrich and Kathleen McGraw. Princeton, NJ: Princeton University Press.

Brambor, Thomas, William Roberts Clark, and Matt Golder. 2006. "Understanding Interaction Models: Improving Empirical Analyses." *Political Analysis* 14: 63–82.

Brooks, Deborah. 2013. *He Runs, She Runs: Why Gender Stereotypes Do Not Harm Women Candidates.* Princeton, NJ: Princeton University Press.

Burrell, Barbara. 1994. *A Woman's Place Is in the House: Campaigning for Congress in the Feminist Era.* Ann Arbor: University of Michigan Press.

Carroll, Susan J., and Kelly Dittmar. 2010. "The 2008 Candidacies of Hillary Clinton and Sarah Palin: Cracking the "Highest, Hardest Glass Ceiling." In *Gender and Elections: Shaping the Future of American Politics,* ed. Susan J. Carroll and Richard L. Fox. New York: Cambridge University Press.

Carsey, Thomas M., and Robert A. Jackson. 2001. "Misreport of Vote Choice in U.S. Senate and Gubernatorial Elections." *State Politics and Policy Quarterly* 1 (2): 196–209.

Cook, Elizabeth Adell, Sue Thomas, and Clyde Wilcox, eds. 1994. *The Year of the Woman: Myths and Realities*. Boulder, CO: Westview Press.

Crump, Matthew J. C., John V. McDonnell, and Todd M. Gureckis. 2013. "Evaluating Amazon's Mechanical Turk as a Tool for Experimental Behavioral Research." *PLoS ONE*.

Darcy, R., Susan Welch, and Janet Clark. 1994. *Women, Elections, and Representation*. 2nd ed. New York: Longman.

Delli Carpini, Michael X., and Scott Keeter. 1996. *What Americans Know about Politics and Why It Matters*. New Haven, CT: Yale University Press.

Ditonto, Tessa. 2017. "A High Bar or a Double Standard? Gender, Competence, and Information in Political Campaigns." *Political Behavior* 39 (2): 301–25.

———. 2018. "A Face Fit for Office? Appearance-Based Competence Inferences in High-Information Environments." *Electoral Studies* 54: 248–53.

Ditonto, Tessa, Allison Hamilton, and David Redlawsk. 2014. "Gender Stereotypes, Information Search and Voting Behavior in Political Campaigns." *Political Behavior* 36 (2): 335–58.

Ditonto, Tessa, and David J. Andersen. 2018. "Two's a Crowd: Women Candidates in Concurrent Elections." *Journal of Women, Politics, & Policy* 39 (3): 257–84.

Dolan, Kathleen. 2004. *Voting for Women: How the Public Evaluates Women Candidates*. Boulder, CO: Westview Press.

———. 2014. *When Does Gender Matter? Women Candidates and Gender Stereotypes in American Elections*. 2014. New York: Oxford University Press.

Duerst-Lahti, Georgia. 2010 "Presidential Elections: Gendered Space and the Case of 2008." In *Gender and Elections: Shaping the Future of American Politics*, ed. Susan J. Carroll and Richard L. Fox. New York: Cambridge University Press.

Eagly, Alice H. 1987. *Sex Differences in Social Behavior: A Social-Role Interpretation*. Hillsdale, NJ: Erlbaum.

Eagly, Alice H., and Steve J. Karau. 2002. "Role Congruity Theory of Prejudice toward Female Leaders." *Psychological Review* 109 (3): 573–98.

Eagly, Alice H., and Wendy Wood. 1982. "Inferred Sex Differences in Status as a Determinant of Gender Stereotypes about Social Influence." *Journal of Personality and Social Psychology* 43: 915–28.

Gaddie, Ronald Keith, and Charles S. Bullock III. 1995. "Congressional Elections and the Year of the Woman: Structural and Elite Influence on Female Candidacies." *Social Science Quarterly* 76 (December): 749–62.

Hayes, Danny. 2011. "When Gender and Party Collide: Stereotyping in Candidate Trait Attribution." *Politics and Gender* 7 (2): 133–65.

Hennings, Valerie, and R. Urbatsch. 2015. "There Can Be Only One (Woman on the Ticket): Gender in Candidate Nominations." *Political Behavior* 37 (3): 749–66.

Holman, Mirya, Jennifer L. Merolla, and Elizabeth J. Zechmeister. 2011. "Sex, Stereotypes, & Security." *Journal of Women, Politics, & Policy* 32 (3): 173–92.

Huddy, Leonie, and Nayda Terkildsen. 1993a. "Gender Stereotypes and the Perception of Male and Female Candidates." *American Journal of Political Science* 37 (1): 119–47.

———. 1993b. "The Consequences for Gender Stereotypes for Women Candidates at Different Levels and Types of Office." *Political Research Quarterly* 46 (3): 503–25.

Huddy, Leonie, and Theresa Capelos. 2002. "The Impact of Gender Stereotypes on Voters' Assessment of Women Candidates." In *Social Psychological Applications to Social Issues: Developments in Political Psychology*. Vol. 5, ed. Victor Ottati. New York: Kluwer Academic/Plenum. 29–53.

Kahn, Kim Fridkin. 1996. *The Political Consequences of Being a Woman: How Stereotypes Influence the Conduct and Consequences of Political Campaigns*. New York: Columbia University Press.

King, David C., and Richard E. Matland. 2003. "Sex and the Grand Old Party: An Experimental Investigation of the Effect of Candidate Sex on Support for a Republican Candidate." *American Politics Research* 31 (6): 595–612.

Koch, Jeffrey W. 2000. "Do Citizens Apply Gender Stereotypes to Infer Candidates' Ideological Orientations?" *Journal of Politics* 62 (2): 414–29.

Krupnikov, Yanna, and Nichole M. Bauer. 2014. "The Relationship Between Campaign Negativity, Gender and Campaign Context." *Political Behavior* 36 (1): 167–88.

Kunda, Ziva, and Steven J. Spencer. 2003. "When Do Stereotypes Come to Mind and When Do They Color Judgment: A Goal-Based Theoretical Framework for Stereotype Activation and Application." *Psychological Bulletin* 129 (4): 522–44.

Lau, Richard R., and David P. Redlawsk. 1997. "Voting Correctly." *American Political Science Review* 91 (3): 585–99.

———. 2001. "Advantages and Disadvantages of Cognitive Heuristics in Political Decision-Making." *American Journal of Political Science* 46 (2): 453–62.

———. 2006. *How Voters Decide: Information Processing during an Election Campaign*. New York: Cambridge University Press.

Lawless, Jennifer L. 2004. "Women, War, and Winning Elections: Gender Stereotyping in the Post–September 11th Era." *Political Research Quarterly* 57 (3): 479–90.

Lawless, Jennifer L., and Kathryn Pearson. 2008. "The Primary Reason for Women's Underrepresentation? Reevaluating Conventional Wisdom." *Journal of Politics* 70 (1): 67–82.

Lawless, Jennifer L., and Richard L. Fox. 2005. *It Takes a Candidate: Why Women Don't Run for Office*. New York: Cambridge University Press.

Leeper, Mark. 1991. "The Impact of Prejudice on Female Candidates: An Experimental Look at Voter Inference." *American Politics Research*. 19 (2): 248–61.

Locksley, A., C. Hepburn, and V. Ortiz. 1982. "Social Stereotypes and Judgments of Individuals: An Instance of the Base-Rate Fallacy." *Journal of Experimental Social Psychology* 18: 23–42.

Locksley, A., E. Borgida, N. Brekke, and C. Hepburn. 1980. "Sex Stereotypes and Social Judgment." *Journal of Personality and Social Psychology* 39 (5): 821–31.

Lupia, Arthur, and Matthew McCubbins. 2000. *Elements of Reason: Cognitions, Choice and the Bounds of Rationality.* Cambridge, UK: Cambridge University Press.

Mullinix, K. J., T. J. Leeper, J. N. Druckman, and J. Freese. 2016. "The Generalizability of Survey Experiments." *Journal of Experimental Political Science* 2 (2): 109–38.

Ono, Yoshikuni, and Barry C. Burden. 2019. "The Contingent Effects of Candidate Sex on Voter Choice." *Political Behavior* 41 (3): 583–607.

Palmer, Barbara, and Dennis Simon. 2008. *Breaking the Political Glass Ceiling: Women and Congressional Elections.* 2nd ed. Abingdon, UK: Routledge Press.

Paolacci, Gabriele, and Jesse Chandler. 2014. "Inside the Turk: Understanding Mechanical Turk as a Participant Tool." *Current Directions in Psychological Science* 23 (3): 184–88.

Plutzer, Eric, and John F. Zipp. 1996. "Identity Politics and Voting for Women Candidates." *Public Opinion Quarterly.* 60 (2): 30–57.

Redlawsk, David. 2004. "What Voters Do: Information Search During Election Campaigns." *Political Psychology* 25 (4): 595–610.

Rosenwasser, Shirley M., and Jana Seale. 1988. "Attitudes Towards a Hypothetical Male of Female Presidential Candidates—A Research Note." *Political Psychology* 9 (4): 591–98.

Sanbonmatsu, Kira. 2006. "Do Parties Know that 'Women Win'? Party Leader Beliefs about Women's Electoral Chances." *Politics & Gender* 2 (4): 431–50.

Sanbonmatsu, Kira, and Kathleen Dolan. 2009. "Do Gender Stereotypes Transcend Party?" *Political Research Quarterly* 62 (3): 485–94.

Schneider, Monica C., and Angela L. Bos. 2013. "Measuring Stereotypes of Female Politicians." *Political Psychology* 35 (2): 245–66.

Sears, David O. 1986. "College Sophomores in the Laboratory: Influences of a Narrow Data Base on Social Psychology's View of Human Nature." *Journal of Personality and Social Psychology* 51 (3): 315–530.

Seltzer, Richard, Jody Newman, and Melissa Voorhees Leighton. 1997. *Sex as a Political Variable: Women as Candidates and Voters in US Elections.* Boulder, CO: Lynn Reinner Publications.

Sinclair, Lisa, and Ziva Kunda. 1999. "Motivated Reasoning with Stereotypes: Activation, Application, and Inhibition." *Psychological Inquiry* 10 (1): 12–22.

Swim, Janet K., Kathryn J. Aikin, and Wayne S. Hall. 1995. "Sexism and Racism:

Old- Fashioned and Modern Prejudices." *Journal of Personality and Social Psychology* 68 (1): 199–214.

Weinberg, Jill D., Jeremy Freese, and David McElhattan. 2014. "Comparing Data Characteristics and Results of an Online Factorial Survey Between a Population-Based and a Crowdsource-Recruited Sample." *Sociological Science* 1: 292–310.

Welch, Susan. 1985. "Are Women More Liberal than Men in the US Congress?" *Legislative Studies Quarterly* 10 (1): 125–34.

Wolak, Jennifer. 2009. "The Consequences of Concurrent Campaigns for Citizen Knowledge of Congressional Candidates." *Political Behavior* 31 (2): 211–29.

Woods, Harriet. 2000. *Stepping Up to Power: The Political Journey of American Women*. Boulder, CO: Westview Press.

Wright, Gerald C. 1990. "Misreports of Vote Choice in the 1988 NES Senate Election Study." *Legislative Studies Quarterly* 15 (4): 543–63.

———. 1993. "Errors in Measuring Vote Choice in the National Election Studies, 1952–88." *American Journal of Political Science* 37 (1): 291–316.

WOMEN IN LEGISLATIVE INSTITUTIONS

GENDERED LEGISLATIVE EFFECTIVENESS IN STATE LEGISLATURES

The Case of Pennsylvania

JENNIE SWEET-CUSHMAN

I n 2014, Pennsylvania State Representative Kate Harper (R) sat in on a hearing about autonomous vehicles. Naturally, the legislators involved were keenly interested in issues of safety and practicality. Like a disproportionate number of daughters and daughters-in-law with adult-caregiving responsibilities, Representative Harper's thoughts went elsewhere. Having cared for an elderly parent herself, Harper immediately wondered whether self-driving cars had the potential to keep seniors in their homes after loss of function would normally resign them to nursing facilities. This was a different perspective, certainly, and one that Harper credits to being a woman with a seat at the legislative table.

Like Representative Harper, scholars of American politics frequently cite the different perspective, life experiences, and skill sets that women bring to the table as legislators, but given women's underrepresentation, the impact can be hard to discern. Indeed, women have always been underrepresented in American politics. This is decidedly true in the Pennsylvania General Assembly, where over only the last two election cycles women have remarkably reached 25% of seats held (Pennsylvania Center for Women and Politics, "Fast Facts") after hovering around 18% for decades. This matters more than just the disproportionate numbers. Research on other legislative bodies has found that when women are elected to office they are more likely to advocate for women's issues, are more successful at guiding legislation through the legislative process, and can help create a more collaborative lawmaking environment (Volden, Wiseman, and Wittmer 2018; Barnello and Bratton 2007; Kathlene 1998; Gagliarducci and Paserman 2016; Anzia and Berry 2011; Cowell-Meyers and Langbein 2009).

I ask whether female legislators are similarly valuable in the Pennsylvania General Assembly by examining legislative effectiveness: the degree to which legislators adeptly perform the entire spectrum of their legislative function, from sponsoring legislation, garnering support, and ultimately steering it towards passage. Pennsylvania provides a fertile ground on which to examine the state legislative environment in this way. It is a full-time, professional legislature and one of the largest in the country. The two political parties have sophisticated (male-dominated) leadership structures and are experiencing partisan polarization on much the same magnitude the country is witnessing at the national level. Furthermore, the masculinized ethos of the institution makes the role of a female legislator both more difficult and more important. In this context, evaluating the role women play in Pennsylvania may have implications for legislatures experiencing these conditions on smaller magnitudes.

Top of mind are women's issues. Since these issues are often thought to be an area of concern to female legislators, one of the questions to address is: How does the underrepresentation of women in Pennsylvania's legislature affect policy for women in the state? I examine gender-based differences, specifically, in support for women's issue bills, and, more generally, women's effectiveness as lawmakers in Pennsylvania, using a number of metrics to illuminate "effectiveness." Partisanship plays a unique role in this legislature in uniting and dividing the women who serve. Women bring unique strengths to policymaking and governing by addressing questions specific to the role of gender in patterns of bill sponsorship in the Pennsylvania General Assembly's 2013–14 legislative term. Women who served in the general assembly at that time when women comprised approximately 18% of the body (Pennsylvania Center for Women and Politics, "Fast Facts") offer unique insights. My analysis reveals that the presence of women in a state legislature may improve the lawmaking process and enhance effectiveness, suggesting state-level lawmaking could be improved by the election of more women to state legislatures.[1]

* * *

JENNIE SWEET-CUSHMAN

Women's Representation in the Keystone State

In Pennsylvania, women's underrepresentation is particularly stark. In the 253-member General Assembly, as of 2019 only 53 female legislators serve in the House, and 13 in the Senate (Pennsylvania Center for Women and Politics, "Fast Facts). This is only somewhat higher than Mississippi, which has the lowest percentage of women-held seats in the country at 13.8%, and pales in comparison to Nevada which, at 50.8%, is the first state to ever have a majority-woman legislature (National Conference of State Legislatures 2019).

Chronic and dramatic underrepresentation of women in Pennsylvania's legislature may be problematic because men and women tend to have different policy preferences. The academic literature on women's representation has consistently revealed how female representatives are more likely than their male counterparts to care about women's issues, sponsor legislation addressing them, and support them with their votes (Volden, Wiseman, and Wittmer 2018), though this finding is generally, as Osborn (2012) states, "complicated" by partisanship, which often means Republican and Democratic women behave very differently.

Given both the paucity of women in Pennsylvania government and the crucial role women appear to play in addressing women's issues, it should be no surprise that Pennsylvania is often criticized for failing to meet the needs of its female citizens. One 2013 study funded by the Center for American Progress, an independent nonpartisan policy institute,[2] gave the state a grade of C-. Other evaluations have given the commonwealth poor ratings as well. A 2015 study by the Institute for Women's Policy Research rated Pennsylvania below average in several categories of public policy for women. Rankings were still worse in a 2016 study conducted by WalletHub (Bernardo 2016).[3]

One way in which Pennsylvania continues to fall behind is economically. Across the United States and in Pennsylvania, women are paid only 80 cents for every dollar a man makes; Pennsylvania ranks twenty-fourth in the country for pay equity (AAUW 2016). Women not only earn less than men for equal employment but are often employed in low-wage jobs (Institute for Women's Policy Research 2015). There are also no laws that require employers to allow mothers to earn paid sick leave (Sweet-Cushman 2015). Pennsylvania is one of twenty-one states that offer no additional family-leave protections beyond those afforded in limited federal law (for example, the Family Medical Leave Act of 1993). Relatedly, Pennsylvania was recently named one of the ten worst states for pregnancy discrimination (Sweet-Cushman 2015). The state has also done little in the way of childcare, an issue crucial to many of Pennsylvania's working mothers; those who do enroll their children in daycare or pre-K have to figure out a complex system of funding (Sweet-Cushman and Harden 2017). It is not surprising that women are disproportionately affected by poverty (National Women's Law Center 2016).

Nowhere are women's issues more divisive in the Commonwealth than in women's reproductive health issues, and the women in the General Assembly are very clear that there are severe differences of opinion among them on issues of and related to abortion. It is difficult for them to discuss, let alone reach compromise, on any issue related to reproductive health. Chu and Posner (2013) point to a number of indicators that women's health needs to be addressed in Pennsylvania: only 36% of the need for publicly funded contraceptive services are being met by publicly supported providers; nearly 11% of nonelderly women are currently uninsured, with restricted access to necessary medical care; and the maternal mortality rate is at 10.1 women per 100,000 live births. While little attention is paid to these concerns for women's health, lawmakers are consistently debating issues surrounding abortion, and legislation on that issue is frequently considered.

Abortion contributes significantly to the disconnect between the Republican and Democratic parties in Pennsylvania, and partisan polarization is a significant problem. Underrepresentation not only affects policy, but also legislative effectiveness, and in a time of increased partisan polarization, women's role may be crucial. Indeed, scholars have demonstrated that polarization may be somewhat counteracted by increasing the representation of women in government, as women are often seen as being more likely to sponsor bipartisan legislation and collaborate compared to their male colleagues (Hawkesworth et al. 2001; Kathlene 1994).

Women Legislating

The most obvious way in which female legislators are thought to govern differently from their male colleagues is that they pay more legislative attention to women's issues (Volden, Wiseman, and Wittmer 2018; Swers 1998; Gerrity, Osborn, and Mendez 2007), which are underrepresented compared to men's issues (Little, Dunn, and Deen 2001). This commitment to women's issues by female legislators exists despite vast differences in other characteristics (Hawkesworth et al. 2001). In fact, Barnello and Bratton (2007) find that gender was the most influential factor in whether a member of a legislature sponsored a women's issue bill. The Center for American Women and Politics (CAWP) (undated) in its report "The Difference Women Make" further highlights how political party did not appear to deter representation of women, and other comprehensive studies have found similar bipartisan efforts to support the policy needs of women (Volden, Wiseman, and Wittmer 2018). Moreover, while Republican women are less likely to pursue women's issues than Democratic women (Osborn 2012), they are still more likely to introduce women's issue legislation compared to Democratic men (Wittmer and Bouché 2013; though see Osborn et al. 2019 for evidence that this pattern may be changing). Women from both parties are more likely to support liberal or moderate positions compared to men (Center for American Women and Politics, "The Difference Women Make"), which has been true of a subset of Republican women in the Pennsylvania General Assembly for many terms.

Indeed, women's distinct contribution to the legislative bodies where they serve is hardly only in the issue priorities they advocate. Female legislators also bring a different approach to governance. Kathlene (1994, 1998) finds that, in the Colorado legislature, female legislators tended to act on a broader, more inclusive, community-oriented basis compared to their male colleagues. Women committee chairs also used their positions to facilitate open discussions among committee members, sponsors, and witnesses whereas their male colleagues use their position to control hearings. More recently, Eisner (2013) examined traits and approaches of contemporary leaders, finding that women were more likely to focus on relationships over tasks. Women tended to encourage showing support for others, creating ideas, and an emphasis on listening to feedback. In contrast, men were more likely to share their power with coworkers and be inspiring leaders as well as placing more value on risk-taking.

Considering the emphasis on connection with others, it is not particularly surprising that women are more engaged in constituency service compared to male colleagues. Thomas (1992) finds that women officeholders spend more hours at their jobs, more hours doing constituency service, and are more likely to regularly meet with constituents compared to male colleagues. One four-state study of state legislators found that women also received more casework requests and were twice as likely to believe that they perform more casework than their colleagues. Female legislators were also three times more likely to agree to perform more casework if they knew they could receive additional resources to do so (Richardson and Freeman 1995).

Collaboration is also often thought to be a key component of women's leadership style. Women emphasize relationships that are empowering, egalitarian, and mutually beneficial as well as emphasizing compromise, consensus building, and cooperation (Cammisa and Reingold 2004). In contrast, men's legislative style is thought to be formal, hierarchical, and more likely to promote authoritative relationships, as well as win-lose: involving conflict, dominance, and manipulation. Women value cooperation, whereas men are believed to be more goal-oriented (Merchant 2012). Men tend to use a task-oriented approach when leading whereas women's leadership style relies heavily on quality of interpersonal relationships.

Collaboration links directly to cosponsorship behavior. Previous research indicates that bills sponsored by female legislators have more cosponsors than those sponsored by men. In fact, women in the US Congress, on average, sponsor three more bills per congress compared to their male colleagues—about 17% more (Anzia and Berry 2011). This legislation also gets more support; women of both parties recruit more cosponsors for their legislation (Gagliarducci and Paserman 2016). Women were not only more likely to attract cosponsors to their own bills but were also more likely to cosponsor bills proposed by colleagues. On average, congresswomen cosponsored twenty-six more bills. At the state level, Holman and Mahoney (2019) find that the presence of a women's caucus is associated with greater collaboration among women, even in the face of increased polarization, but only when the institution is controlled by Democrats.[4]

Despite their productivity as legislators, legislation sponsored by women still faces some obstacles. Bills sponsored by women appeared to have fewer cosponsors from the opposite party (Gagliarducci and Paserman 2016). Support of male colleagues may also be key, in particular, to the success of legislation addressing women's issues. Wittmer and Bouché (2013) find that, when both male and female legislators work on address-

JENNIE SWEET-CUSHMAN

ing women's issues, states adopt more women-friendly policies. Specifically, female sponsorship alone does lead to an increase in a state's support for women's issues, unless men are underrepresented as cosponsors. In this case, the legislation is less likely to be passed (Wittmer and Bouché 2013). In Congress, too, women's issues are more likely to pass if they are sponsored by men (Volden, Wiseman, Wittmer 2018). Essentially, it appears that the optimal legislative environment for addressing women's issues is a near gender parity of legislators promoting these issues and participating in coalitions.

The impact of representation is truly felt only if women are successful in their legislative efforts. Empirical evidence mostly finds that they are. Women are not only more likely to introduce legislation regarding women, children, and families, but they are also more likely to successfully steer this legislation compared to their male colleagues (Thomas 1991). Cowell-Meyers and Langbein (2009) found that the increased presence of women in state legislatures increased the likelihood of success in passing legislation in some of these policy areas. Similarly, Saint-Germain (1989) found female legislators in Arizona were more successful than men at enacting their proposals, regardless of the policy area. Studies of Congress have shown similar patterns for legislation sponsored by women (Swers 1998), indicating that these patterns hold across levels of government. Women in Congress have been shown to sponsor and pass more legislation and procure more federal funds for their districts than male representatives (Anzia and Berry 2011). Not all research is as conclusive about women's effectiveness as lawmakers. Volden, Wiseman, and Wittmer's examination of the US House of Representatives over the past four decades calls into question the power of women's legislative specialization. Most notably, on bills related to health or education, women were actually less successful than men who sponsored this legislation.

While women may be more effective at passing legislation, it is not clear how they handle claiming credit for their legislative work. A recent study revealed that male legislators were no more likely to claim credit for legislative accomplishments compared to their female colleagues, but that women are more likely to attribute success to their efforts at collaboration (Allen 2016). Another study, however, looking at newsletters produced by members of the 107th Congress, found that women are more likely to claim credit for their accomplishments (Dolan and Kropf 2004). Other research has offered a contradictory take, finding that male senators were more likely to claim credit for work on both women's and men's issues (Thomas 2005). Many, though not all of these studies about women's legislative performance, focus on the congressional level. While studying Congress offers insights about the effectiveness of female lawmakers at the national level, it is not clear if these insights always extend to state legislatures.

To build and extend upon previous research on women's performance in legislative institutions, I apply theories of women's legislative performance at the state level, specifically the case of Pennsylvania. Generalizing scholarship about Congress to the state level has proven to be only partially instructive in how gender dynamics affect legislating in subnational bodies. Do women in Pennsylvania's general assembly behave like their co-partisans in polarized Washington, DC? This is not the first attempt to measure women's legislative performance in state legislatures (see, for example, Osborn 2012). Each state legislature faces a unique set of constraints, and using Pennsylvania as a case study allows me to glean whether the behavior of women in other states, such as Iowa, extend to Pennsylvania. The insights offered here have implications for women's representation in subnational institutions. The policies implemented at the state level frequently have a direct and immediate impact on the lives of women, men, and children in a particular state.

Methodology

I consider gendered aspects of lawmaking in the Pennsylvania context using a mixed-methods approach. First, I use bill-sponsorship data collected from the Pennsylvania state legislative database for the 2013–14 legislative term. During this term, eight women served in the Senate (5D, 3R) and thirty-seven in the House (16D, 21R) (Pennsylvania Center for Women and Politics, "Fast Facts"). Of these, only six (2D, 4R) chaired committees. In all, more than 3,800 bills were evaluated, approximately 1,400 Senate bills and 2,400 House bills. Bills were coded by sponsorship, topic, and degree of legislative success, in an effort to examine the role female legislators play in lawmaking. For each bill, data gathered included: bill number, bill title, date introduced, status of bill, date passed, days on legislative agenda, and last day of activity. Primary sponsor gender, party, sponsor district, and years of service were also included. Overall, men sponsored a majority of bills (86%). I also coded patterns of cosponsorship in the bill-sponsorship data. The average number of cosponsors on a bill was 17.2, though numbers of cosponsors varied greatly, from only 1 to as many as 110.

Each bill was given a primary code based on whether the legislative topic was a women's issue or not. Women's issues are a diverse set of topics, so two independent coders coded the women's bills into subcategories.[5] Coders used Swers's (2002) classification system and divided the bills into three categories: feminist, social welfare, and antifeminist. Those classified as feminist bills included bills that protected victims of domestic violence or sexual assault; expanded family and medical leave; promoted gender equality and antidiscrimination in areas such as housing, education, and employment; created programs for women-owned businesses; or promoted funding for women's health (Swers 2002).[6] Those categorized as social welfare bills included issues such as expanding health insurance, establishing regulations for adoption or child support, and punishing crimes against the elderly and children (Swers 2002).[7] Antifeminist bills were those that inhibited role equality or gender equality.[8] I added a subset labeled "other" for bills that did not fall into the other three subsets. All bills were given a primary code (women's v. other) and secondary code (topic). The modal legislative topics were budget/financial/taxes, which included 572 bills (14.8%) and crime/judicial with 561 bills (14.5%)—both topics were not considered women's issues. Republican female legislators, in particular, emphasized this reality; as Representative Donna Oberlander (R) said, she is very conscious that she represents both the men and the women in her district, so she thinks more broadly about the legislative priorities she champions. Only about 6% of all bills introduced were classified as women's issues (n = 231). Most of these bills were classified as social welfare legislation (73%).

Next, I conducted semi-structured in-person interviews with twelve members who had served during the session being analyzed. Ten of these interviews were with members of the House and were split evenly between women belonging to each party (5R, 5D). The other two were with members of the senate, again equally representing both parties (1R, 1D). The questions mirrored those explored quantitatively: issue priorities, women's leadership and governing styles, collaborations, and bipartisanship among women in the legislature.

Findings

In many ways, the women of Pennsylvania's General Assembly are much like those who have been previously studied in the US Congress and other state legislatures. They were more likely than men to sponsor women's legislation, be collaborative in their efforts (both with other women and with the other party), and less likely to claim credit for their accomplishments.

Women's Issues. In the legislative session I analyzed, of all the bills sponsored by women, 40.6% were considered women's bills, whereas only 32.8% ($p < 0.05$) of bills sponsored by men fit into this category. This supports previous research that suggests women are more likely than their male colleagues to sponsor women's issue bills. While men were the primary sponsor of more individual pieces of legislation, as a percentage of their representation, women were much more likely to sponsor feminist legislation. Notably, while more of these feminist bills were sponsored by Democrats (35), Republicans were primary sponsors on 23 of them.[9]

Many of the female legislators interviewed were quick to point out that they do not see women's issues as their only, or even primary, focus as legislators. Much like Representative Oberlander (R), Representative Tina Pickett (R) emphasized that her success as a legislator is primarily because she considers the needs of all her constituents, nearly half of whom are male. Representative Becky Corbin (R) is similarly focused on providing excellent constituent service to individuals in her district—a focus that has no gender consideration. Nonetheless, many of the Democrats (and some Republicans) interviewed felt very strongly that they had an obligation to stand up for the needs of women in the legislature. Representative Maria Donatucci (D) in particular emphasized that she absolutely prioritizes women's issues in her legislative agenda and expressed significant concern over partisan battles that have shut down discussion on many of these issues.

Representative Madeleine Dean (D) expressed a concern that many had: divisions around the issue of abortion make other non-abortion issues difficult to discuss. The women in the legislature are just as divided as the men (primarily along partisan lines) on this issue and, as Dean suggested, it lessens the depth of solidarity in the women's caucus. As a result, other issues that concern women don't always get the attention or consideration they deserve. She cited the minimum wage as an issue that

JENNIE SWEET-CUSHMAN

has significant implications for women but felt that many of the men serving in the legislature might not appreciate the impact.

Women on both sides of the aisle expressed concern about focusing too much on women's issues. Representative Mauree Gingrich (R) said she understood that women needed to tackle these issues or no one else would, but that female legislators needed to make it clear that they "brought more to the table" than just advocacy for women's issues. For Representative Mary Jo Daley (D), that means finding common ground is crucial because it allows a dialogue on issues that can improve the lives of women even if they are not explicitly women's issues (for example, rental agreements). Representative Margo Davidson (D) is very committed to the idea that solidarity among the women on both sides of the legislature can mean more progress on issues that are of critical importance to women, including children, family, and elderly issues. She believes leveraging the priorities of her women colleagues helps move these issues forward.

Collaboration. In Pennsylvania, then, if female legislators of both parties tend to rely more heavily than their male colleagues on collaboration, should we expect legislation introduced by women in the Pennsylvania General Assembly to attract more cosponsors than legislation sponsored by the men? To address this question, the relationship between gender and cosponsorship was examined. This analysis finds that Pennsylvania's female legislators had an average of 18.2 cosponsors, compared to their male colleagues, who had an average of 17.1 cosponsors ($p < 0.05$). The results further reflect the findings of Gagliarducci and Paserman's (2016) study which found that female legislators recruit larger numbers of cosponsorship on their bills compared to male colleagues.

There was little disagreement on women's leadership style among the women in the General Assembly with whom I spoke. Everyone tended to see women as working differently from their male colleagues. Senator Judy Schwank (D) and Representative Margo Davidson (D) remarked that they often say women legislate differently, that they start their career with goals and work towards those goals very pragmatically, looking immediately for like-minded legislators to join their efforts. Representative Tina Pickett (R) likened it to how women juggle the many different demands of a household—they multitask. Representative Pam Snyder (D) agreed that the women have a handle on "everything" while men focus on very particular things.

One aspect of the job women seemed to have a firm grasp on was constituent service. Representative Becky Corbin (R) proudly reported that she prioritizes constituency service more than introducing and cosponsoring legislation. In fact, Representative Corbin, known as a "Green Republican" in the state, was known for prioritizing the environmental needs of her constituents, and voting with Democrats against the will of her caucus.

Corbin's willingness to compromise with Democrats on environmental issues is only one example. The emphasis on collaboration by women is also accentuated by their tendency to reach across party lines. Researchers found that female politicians' approach to cooperation, conciliation, and consensus building was vastly different from a male legislator's often solitary competitive approach (Donaldson 2011). The focus on consensus building by female legislators was particularly strong for women in the minority party (Gagliarducci and Paserman 2016). Women, generally, are more likely to reach across party lines to find support for the issue priorities—particularly if they are in the minority.

Analyzing sex and cosponsorship by party, there is evidence that women are more likely to cosponsor bills that were sponsored by the opposing party. In the minority, the Democratic side, female legislators had slightly more Republican cosponsors for legislation they sponsored than did their male Democratic colleagues (3.5 Republican cosponsors v. 3 Republican cosponsors, respectively; $p < 0.05$). Republicans, who were in the majority during the term examined, unsurprisingly attracted more support for legislation they proposed. Republican men had on average 7.2 cosponsors for legislation they introduced, while Republican women averaged 8.5 cosponsors on their legislation ($p < 0.05$). Women in both parties demonstrate a greater ability to attract fellow legislators to support their legislation (see figure 7.1).

The idea that women would be more collaborative legislators came as no surprise to most of the female legislators I interviewed. Many of them spoke of the women in the legislature as being more cooperative than their male colleagues, with at least one mentioning how crucial women's flexibility is in a legislature increasingly divided by partisan rigidity. Many of the women, primarily Democrats (but not exclusively so), proudly referenced how women worked together—often across party lines—with other women to move legislation forward. Senator Judy Schwank (D) pointed to women's health concerns that brought women from both parties to-

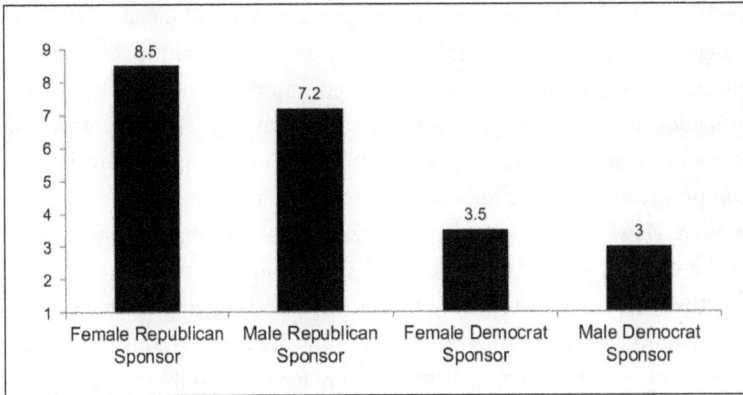

Figure 7.1. Number of Opposing Partisan Cosponsors on Bills

gether, in particular a domestic violence bill she and other female legislators helped pass when it would have otherwise died. She views women as more "pragmatic," and this flexibility helps them navigate obstacles that might otherwise prevent progress. Representative Mauree Gingrich (R) emphasized this flexibility as a plus for women, noting that compromise happens when women are leading, "not just from the front, but from the middle and back," as well.

Representative Donna Oberlander (R) felt the collaboration with other women happens very naturally, with or without a formal caucus, because women are apt to band together around common ground, and being a woman is one more place female legislators have common ground. Representative Maria Donatucci (D), who is very supportive of the idea of a formal women's caucus, stressed how it creates a forum for women to leverage this solidarity because it "opens something up" when they are having discussions, and Representative Margo Davidson (D) explicitly described many of the female legislators having an informal pact to support one another's efforts. Were it not for issues around women's reproductive health dividing them, there would—theoretically—be even greater potential for collaboration within the women's caucus. Many legislators expressed frustration that abortion issues consistently obstruct opportunities to deal with less controversial issues facing women.

Several legislators pointed to a high-profile example of the impact of polarization: the five-month-long budget impasse Pennsylvania experienced in 2015 (Russ 2016). The impasse was a prolonged battle over budget priorities between the Democratic governor and the Republican-controlled legislature. This delay affected school districts, colleges, and other social service agencies, which found themselves having to take out loans or even close due to lack of funding (Russ 2016). Clearly, lack of compromise has had an impact on Pennsylvania's ability to pass state legislation. However, many state legislators spoke to how many of the women of the General Assembly on both sides of the aisle started having coffee together before sessions during this tense period—giving them a unique opportunity to discuss, brainstorm, and consider paths to concession. Until this most recent term in Pennsylvania, female Republican legislators have consistently outnumbered female Democratic legislators (Pennsylvania Center for Women and Politics, "Fast Facts"), but nationally, women of both parties appear more likely to reach across party lines in order to reach a consensus (Gagliarducci and Paserman 2013).

However, Representative Tina Pickett (R) emphasized that the solidarity among women wasn't necessarily the most crucial component of generating support—even for women's issues. Women in the legislature are also rational actors who draw on collaborations across regional alliances and trusted relationships to accomplish their legislative goals.

EFFECTIVENESS AND CREDIT CLAIMING

I also examine whether Pennsylvania's legislative women are more or less effective at moving legislation through the legislative process. More narrowly, will female legislators will be more likely to effectively sponsor bills related to traditional "women's issues" such as childcare or healthcare in comparison to traditional "men's issues" such as transportation or financial/taxes?

Effectiveness. Generally, Pennsylvania's female legislators do appear to be somewhat more effective at successfully steering legislation through the legislative process compared to their male colleagues. Of the bills passed in the 2013–14 session, female legislators had a higher average percentage of their sponsored bills passed (9.7%), compared to their male counterparts (9%). In part, individual legislators who were quite successful in getting their sponsored legislation onto the governor's desk drove this higher rate for women. Representative Kate Harper (R), for example, passed four of her sponsored bills during this session. The results, in this case, further support previous research suggesting that female legislators can be more successful at getting legislation passed.

There is also evidence that female legislators are focusing these efforts on issues of importance to women. Nearly half of the bills sponsored by women that were passed and signed into law by the governor (49%) were women's issue bills. In contrast, only 29.5% of male legislator's successful legislation dealt with women's issues ($p < 0.001$).

Representative Harper, with 16 years of service under her belt, was quick to point out how seniority affects women's effectiveness. Out of the bills primarily sponsored by women, the six women whose tenure had elevated them to chairing a committee sponsored more than one in ten of them. This is an important consideration given that women in the Pennsylvania General Assembly have, on average, less seniority. The men serving during the 2013–14 term had, on average, almost 2.5 more years of service than their female counterparts. Representative Gingrich (R) recognized this strength as well, suggesting that others (and presumably men) couldn't "bully seniority."

But other women suggested that a strong work ethic, ability to multitask, and a focus on a broader set of legislative issues played a part. Senator Camera Bartolotta (R) felt that being a woman could be a real advantage given women's tendency to study and work hard, which—she believes—is recognized, and respected. Representative Mary Jo Daley (D) emphasized the importance of being a pragmatist in the legislature—a trait she thought women were more likely to bring to their legislative efforts. Pragmatism was mentioned by virtually every woman legislator I spoke to as a key ingredient in all aspects of their success as legislators.

Credit Claiming. My interviews with female legislators in the Pennsylvania General Assembly offered some insight into why making claims about how gender affects credit claiming could be difficult. While this study's data clearly *formally* identified who passed legislation and who, among their colleagues on both sides of the aisle, supported these efforts, the data miss one significant contribution to lawmaking that many of the women interviewed identified. Nearly all of the legislators said that women were more likely to shop their legislation (or ideas for legislation) around to legislators who might be more successful in passing it. In some cases, this was women in the minority approaching those in the majority for sponsorship—a common strategy for male and female legislators.

However, many women noted that they had "given" legislation to a male colleague who they knew would have better success, and several women spoke with thoughtful resignation about male colleagues who took their legislation, put their names on it, and passed it without recognizing their contribution. It isn't clear how common this sort of behavior might be, but most of the female legislators I talked to recognized that it is something that happens with some frequency and with a gendered consideration. The bill-sponsorship data, then, may actually underestimate the influence women are having in the General Assembly. Significantly, few seemed to care that they might be denied credit for their own legislative work. For the women of the Pennsylvania General Assembly, the goal is to get things done, not to find some glory in doing so.

In summary, I find evidence of gendered effectiveness in legislating in the Pennsylvania General Assembly in that female legislators demonstrate three legislative behaviors that add real benefit to the legislative process. First, women's issues get greater attention from female legislators, so women receive better policy representation. Second, women work more collaboratively. They work with other women to accomplish legislative goals and with members of the other party more frequently than their male counterparts. And third, women are more likely to get their legislation signed into law, though their relative reluctance to claim credit may mean this is an overly conservative measure of their success in the legislature.

What If We Elected More Women?

I don't care whether my bill comes forward. I don't care if *my* name is on it if I can help it get done. That is my philosophy, maybe even to a fault.

—REPRESENTATIVE MADELEINE DEAN (D)

Representative Madeleine Dean (D), who has recently become one of the very few women ever elected to the US Congress from Pennsylvania, articulates well a common theme among the women of the Pennsylvania General Assembly: they are willing to do the work whether or not they

JENNIE SWEET-CUSHMAN

get credit for it. By all the measures examined here, the group of female legislators in the General Assembly could be aptly described as small, but mighty. While some of the gender-based differences are small, they speak to the importance of women's presence—much like Mahoney's essay highlights regarding sexual harassment in her contribution to this volume. In both the data and our interviews with legislators, I find that women are more likely to sponsor women's issues, have a more collaborative legislative style, and be more effective at passing legislation—including legislation dealing with women's issues. My interviews also suggest that women may be less interested in claiming credit for their accomplishments.

These findings are consistent with a host of political science research that points to women's effectiveness as legislators—both at the state and at the national level. It would appear female legislators in the Pennsylvania General Assembly are cast from a similar mold, bringing enhanced effectiveness, policy responsiveness, and more collaboration to the table. These findings, however, leave open a question crucial to good governance in our state legislatures: *What if we elected more women?*

Notes

1. The author would like to than the many research assistants who worked on data collection, coding, and researching for this project, including Ashley Harden, Lauren Schlegel, and Hali Santiago. The Pennsylvania Center for Women and Politics sponsored and funded this research.

2. The study examined thirty-six factors related to the economy, leadership, and health of Pennsylvanians in an attempt to provide a deeper examination of disparities for women within the state.

3. WalletHub is a credit-improvement website which hires research analysts to conduct studies to increase transparency with its consumers.

4. Pennsylvania does not officially have a women's caucus in either chamber of its legislature, but a Women's Health Caucus, formed in 2015 by a bipartisan gender-inclusive group of legislators, has functioned to break down some of the rancor around abortion policy in the state. Women in the legislature also noted in their interviews that the women think of themselves of a "caucus" when they work together.

5. Intercoder reliability was examined using Cohen's Kappa = 874, $p < 0.05$. Inconsistencies were later resolved by discussion between the coders.

6. An example of a bill categorized in this subset was "An Act amending the act of October 27, 1955 (P.L.744, No. 222), known as the Pennsylvania Human Relations Act, further providing for findings and declaration of policy, for right to freedom from discrimination in employment, housing and public accommodation, for definitions, for unlawful discriminatory practices and for powers and duties of the commission."

7. This subset included bills such as "An Act amending Title 18 (Crimes and Offenses) of the Pennsylvania Consolidated Statutes, further providing for the offense of endangering welfare of children."

8. These bills often focused on abortion or attempted to limit the coverage of oral contraceptives. An example would be "An Act ensuring the rights of conscience of Pennsylvania citizens relating to health insurance; and providing for health insurance coverage limitations for contraception, sterilization and abortifacient drugs and devices."

9. All antifeminist bills were sponsored by Republican male legislators.

References

AAUW. 2016. "The Simple Truth about the Gender Pay Gap (Fall 2016)." www.aauw .org/research/the-simple-truth-about-the-gender-pay-gap/ (accessed January 2, 2017).

Allen, Amanda. 2016. "The Priorities and Accomplishments of Kentucky Legislators: Is There a Gender Difference?" Senior honors thesis. College of Arts and Sciences, University of Louisville.

Anzia, Sarah, and Christopher Berry. 2011. "The Jackie (and Jill) Robinson Effect: Why Do Congresswomen Outperform Congressmen?" *American Journal of Political Science* 55 (3): 478–93.

Atkinson, Melanie L., and Jason H. Windett. 2015. "Electoral Security and the Strategic Legislative Behavior of Women in Congress." 1–30.

Barnello, Michelle, and Kathleen Bratton. 2007. "Bridging the Gender Gap in Bill Sponsorship." *Legislative Studies Quarterly* 3 (3): 449–74.

Bernardo, Richie. 2016. "2016's Best & Worst States for Women's Equality." August 23. wallethub.com/edu/best-and-worst-states-for-women-equality/5835/ (accessed December 2, 2016).

Caiazza, Amy. 2004. "Does Women's Representation in Elected Office Lead to Women-Friendly Policy? Analysis of State-Level Data." *Women & Politics* 26 (1): 35–70.

Cammisa, Anne, and Beth Reingold. 2004. "Women in State Legislatures and State Legislative Research: Beyond Sameness and Difference." *State Politics & Policy Quarterly* 4 (2): 181–210.

Carroll, Susan. 2000. "Representing Women: Congresswomen's Perceptions of Their Representational Roles." April 13. www.capwip.org/readingroom/cong roles.pdf (November 23, 2016).

Center for American Women and Politics. Undated. "The Difference Women Make." cawp.rutgers.edu/sites/default/files/resources/the_difference_women _make_-_2013.pdf (accessed November 2, 2016).

———. Undated. "Women in the U.S. Congress 2019." www.cawp.rutgers.edu/women -us-congress-2019 (accessed March 20, 2019).

———. Undated. "Women State Legislators: Past, Present and Future." www.cawp
.rutgers.edu/sites/default/files/resources/stlegpastpresent future.pdf (accessed
November 2, 2016).

Chu, Anna, and Charles Posner. 2013. "The State of Women in America: A 50-State
Analysis of How Women Are faring Across the Nation." September. www.ameri
canprogress.org/wp-content/uploads/2013/09/StateOfWomenReport.pdf
(accessed December 2, 2016).

Cowell-Meyers, Kimberly, and Laura Langbein. 2009. "Linking Women's Descriptive and Substantive Representation in the United States." *Politics & Gender*
5 (4): 491–518.

Dolan, Julie, and Jonathan Kropf. 2004. "Credit Claiming from the U.S. House
Gendered Communication Styles?" *Press/Politics* 9 (1): 41–59.

Donaldson, Leah. 2011. "Female Legislators in the United States and Rhode Island."
Roger Williams University Law Review 16 (2): 278–304.

Eagly, Alice, Amanda Diekman, Mary Johannesen-Schmidt, and Anne Koenig.
2004. "Gender Gaps in Sociopolitical Attitudes: A Social Psychological Analysis." *Journal of Personality and Social Psychology* 87 (6): 796–816.

Eisner, Susan. 2013. "Leadership: Gender and Executive Style." *SAM Advanced
Management Journal* 78 (1): 26–41.

Gagliarducci, Stefano, and Daniele Paserman. 2013. "Gender Differences in Cooperative Environments: Evidence from the US Congress." portal.idc.ac.il/en
/schools/economics/homepage/documents/gendercooperativeness_june2013
_v1_all.pdf (accessed November 28, 2016).

———. 2016. "Gender Differences in Cooperative Environments: Evidence from
the US Congress." www.econstor.eu/bitstream/10419/145262/1/dp10128.pdf
(accessed November 28, 2016).

Gerrity, Jessica, Tracy Osborn, and Jeanette Mendez. 2007. "Women and Representation: A Different View of the District?" *Politics & Gender* 3 (2): 179–200.

Hawkesworth, Mary, Kathleen Casey, Krista Jenkins, and Kathrine Kleeman. 2001.
"Legislating by and for Women: A Comparison of the 103rd and 104th Congress." November. www.cawp.rutgers.edu/sites/default/files/resources/cong
report103-104.pdf (accessed November 28, 2016).

Holman, M. R., and A. Mahoney. 2019. "Stop, Collaborate, and Listen: Women's
Collaboration in US State Legislatures." *Legislative Studies Quarterly* 43 (2):
179–206.

Institute for Women's Policy Research. 2015. "The Status of Women in the States
2015." May. www.iwpr.org/publications/pubs/the-status-of-women-in-the
-states-2015-full-report (accessed December 2, 2016).

Kathlene, Lyn. 1994. "Power and Influence in State Legislative Policy-Making: The
Interaction of Gender and Position in Committee Hearing Debates." *American
Political Science Review* 88: 560–76.

———. 1998. "In a Different Voice: Women and the Policy Process." In *Women and Elective Office: Past, Present, and Future,* ed. Sue Thomas and Clyde Wilcox. New York: Oxford University Press.

Little, Thomas, Dana Dunn, and Rebecca Deen. 2001. "A View from the Top: Gender Differences in Legislative Priorities Among State Legislative Leaders." *Women & Politics* 22 (4): 29–50.

Manning, Jennifer, Ida Brudnick, and Colleen Shogan. 2015. "Women in Congress: Historical Overview, Tables, and Discussion." April 29. www.fas.org/sgp/crs/misc/R43244.pdf (accessed November 28, 2016).

Merchant, Karima. 2012. "How Men and Women Differ: Gender Differences in Communication Styles, Influence Tactics, and Leadership Styles." December 3. scholarship.claremont.edu/cgi/viewcontent.cgi?article=1521&context=cmc_theses (accessed November 28, 2016).

National Conference of State Legislatures. 2016. "Women in State Legislatures for 2016." www.ncsl.org/legislators-staff/legislators/womens-legislative-network/women-in-state-legislatures-for-2016.aspx (accessed November 2, 2016).

———. 2019. "Women in State Legislatures for 2019." www.ncsl.org/legislators-staff/legislators/womens-legislative-network/women-in-state-legislatures-for-2019.aspx (accessed March 20, 2019).

National Women's Law Center. 2016. "Women and Poverty, State by State." September 15. nwlc.org/resources/women-and-poverty-state-state/ (accessed January 2, 2017).

Osborn, Tracy L. 2012. *How Women Represent Women: Political Parties, Gender, and Representation in the State Legislatures.* New York: Oxford University Press.

Osborn, T., R. J. Kreitzer, E. U. Schilling, and J. Hayes Clark. 2019. "Ideology and Polarization Among Women State Legislators." *Legislative Studies Quarterly.*

Pennsylvania Center for Women and Politics. Undated. "Fast Facts Pennsylvania." www.chatham.edu/pcwp/research/fastfacts.cfm (accessed January 16, 2017).

———. Undated. "State." www.chatham.edu/pcwp/research/elective-office.cfm (accessed November 2, 2016).

Representation 2020. 2016. "Gender Parity Index." www.representation2020.com/gender-parity-index (accessed January 2, 2017).

Richardson, Lilliard, and Patricia Freeman. 1995. "Gender Differences in Constituency Service among State Legislators." *Political Research Quarterly* 48 (1): 169–79.

Russ, Hilary. 2016. "Pennsylvania Governor to Veto Latest Budget as Stalemate Drags On." March 16. www.reuters.com/article/us-pennsylvania-budget-idUSKCN0WI319 (accessed January 16, 2017).

Saint-Germain, Michelle. 1989. "Does Their Difference Make a Difference? The Impact of Women on Public Policy in the Arizona Legislature." *Social Science Quarterly* 70 (4): 956–68.

Sanbonmatsu, Kira. Undated. "Why Women? The Impact of Women in Elective Office." www.politicalparity.org/wp-content/uploads/2015/08/Parity-Research -Women-Impact.pdf (accessed November 2, 2016).

Sweet-Cushman, Jennie. 2015. "FMLA in PA: Analysis of Family and Medical Leave Policy in the State." *Commonwealth.* November.

Sweet-Cushman, Jennie, and Ashley Harden. 2017. "Is This the Care We Need? An Examination of Childcare Policy in Pennsylvania." *Commonwealth* 19, no. 2.

Swers, Michele. 1998. "Are Women More Likely to Vote for Women's Issue Bills than Their Male Colleagues?" *Legislative Studies Quarterly* 23 (3): 435–48.

———. 2002. *The Difference Women Make: The Policy Impact of Women in Congress.* Chicago: University of Chicago Press.

Thomas, Sue. 1991. "The Impact of Women on State Legislative Policies." *Journal of Politics* 53 (4): 958–76.

———. 1992. "The Effects of Race and Gender on Constituency Serve." *Western Political Quarterly* 45 (1): 169–80.

———. 2005. *Women and Elective Office: Past, Present, and Future.* 2nd ed. New York: Oxford University Press.

Volden, Craig, Alan Wiseman, and Dana Wittmer. 2018. "Women's Issues and Their Fates in the US Congress." *Political Science Research and Methods* 6 (4): 679–96.

Whistler, Donald and Mark Ellickson. 2011. "Women and Men's Legislative Success in 21st Century Professional and Citizen State Legislatures." *American Review of Politics* 32: 213–31.

Wittmer, Dana, and Vanessa Bouché. 2013. "The Limits of Gendered Leadership: Policy Implications of Female Leadership on 'Women's Issues.'" *Politics & Gender* 9 (3): 245–75.

#METOO IN THE STATE HOUSE

ANNA MITCHELL MAHONEY, MEGHAN KEARNEY, AND CARLY MEGAN SHAFFER

I n May 2013, the Iowa Senate communications director, Kirsten Anderson, complained of unwelcome harassment at work. She was subsequently fired, mere hours after the complaint was received. In response to her suspicious dismissal, Anderson sued the state and asked other staffers and legislators to write depositions to support her case (Wing 2013). In October 2018, the depositions from the Anderson case were released to the public, revealing a toxic and pervasive culture of sexual harassment in the legislature, including inappropriate and overtly sexual, misogynistic, and homophobic comments; repeated touching of women without their consent; and a suffocating patriarchal culture in the Iowa statehouse.

The problems in the Iowa General Assembly are common not just for state legislators but for workers across industries. In 2007, activist Tarana Burke created Just Be Inc., a nonprofit organization that helps victims of sexual harassment and assault, and launched MeToo on Myspace as a tool to connect them to resources (Garcia 2017; Harris 2018). On October 15, 2017, #MeToo went viral when tweeted by actress Alyssa Milano in the wake of the Harvey Weinstein scandal, wherein a powerful Hollywood producer was accused of multiple instances of harassment and assault (Garcia 2017). The #MeToo movement also had a large impact on state politics. The Associated Press reported that 76 state legislators were accused of sexual misconduct between October 2017 and August 2018 with at least 27 remaining on the ballot in 2018 and 19 surviving their primaries (Norwood 2018).

Scholars have demonstrated the gendered barriers for women seeking public office (Bauer 2015; Carroll and Fox 2012; Carroll and Sanbonmatsu 2013; Ditonto 2017; Ditonto and Andersen in this volume; Dittmar

2015) as well as the marginalization they face once inside the legislature (Brown 2014; Erikson and Josefsson 2018; Hawkesworth 2003; Mahoney 2018). Winning election to public office does not shield female legislators from the same harassment faced by women working in the private sector. In fact, like women in other male-dominated fields, female legislators may be particularly vulnerable to such behavior (Parker 2018; Krook 2017). In describing political institutions as gendered, Sally J. Kenney argues: "Although some state legislators are part-time or unpaid, and despite the distinctive features of political institutions, courtrooms, defense departments, embassies, and statehouses are workplaces, peopled by those in pursuit of a career. . . . Gender is continually produced in the workplace rather than something existing, stable, and fully formed, prior to one's entry into it" (1996).

Sexual harassment, a gendered practice wherein (mostly) men exploit a power imbalance over (mostly) women due to gender hierarchies, can proliferate within deeply gendered legislatures where women are marginalized from positional and informal power and where relationships are currency (Berdahl 2007a; Duerst-Lahti 2002). In fact, evidence suggests that harassment is used as a tool to put in their place those women who have transgressed that power dynamic by achieving leadership positions (Berdahl 2007b; Hawkesworth 2019; McLaughlin, Uggen, and Blackstone 2012; Rudman et al. 2012)[1] where "they may be viewed and treated in a hostile way precisely because of their manifest competence" (Manne 2017).[2]

While women may organize collectively to counteract this marginalization, backlash may result as a consequence of such organizing (Barnes 2016; Mahoney 2018). Globally, women's ability to shape the legislatures in which they work has been dependent on many factors, including the proportion of women in office, structural features like quotas, and levels of backlash from their male colleagues (O'Brien and Piscopo 2018). Regardless of the role female legislators can play in changing their workplace cultures, legislative leaders are ultimately responsible for protecting citizens, staffers, lobbyists, and legislators from all forms of discrimination, including sexual harassment.

Our research questions are: What sexual harassment policies exist for those working in US state legislatures? What are the characteristics of these policies, and do they adhere to best practices? Are all workers (lobbyists, legislators, and staff) covered by the policies and held accountable for their behavior? How are elected officials, in particular, held accountable by these policies? As political institutions, are legislatures able to adequately adjudicate this type of workplace discrimination? We provide some background information on the evolution of sexual harassment policies and prevention in general before specifically describing the prevalence of policies in the fifty US state legislatures. We report the nature of these policies and how states measure up to best practices as recommended by the National Conference of State Legislatures. Finally, we discuss how even the best practices in sexual harassment policy fall short and how legislatures as political institutions may be uniquely challenged in holding perpetrators accountable.

The Evolution of US Sexual Harassment Policy

Although sexual harassment has a long history, sexual harassment policy is a relatively new phenomenon. The Equal Employment Opportunity Commission (EEOC), under the aegis of the Civil Rights Act of 1964, first articulated a legal definition of sexual harassment in the United States in 1980. Two types of sexual harassment were broadly outlined: quid pro quo harassment and a hostile environment. Quid pro quo harassment consists of attempts to extort sexual favors through threats of negative consequences or bribes of promotion or other workplace perks. A hostile environment is a space characterized by pervasive unwanted or offensive verbal or physical conduct that makes the recipient feel unsafe or unwelcome (Fitzgerald 1993). Current EEOC statistics state that 7,609 charges of sexual harassment were filed in fiscal year 2018, a 12% increase from 2017. Further, the EEOC filed 41 sexual harassment lawsuits, a 50% increase from 2017.[3]

Feminist theory regards sexual harassment as a consequence of gender inequality manifesting in exertions of power that disadvantage women (MacKinnon 1979). The theory of gendered institutions would suggest that sexual harassment is not just a result of bad apples and individualized behaviors, but a consequence of the underlying structures and norms that characterize these institutions marginalizing women and placing men at the top of the hierarchy (Britton 2000; Hawkesworth 2003; Kenney 1996). In male-dominated workplaces, like legislatures, "the harasser uses sexualized and nonsexualized conduct to construct the harassed woman as an outsider in the workplace—de-authorized and denigrated, in her own eyes and in the eyes of others" (Siegel 2004). Inadequate sexual harassment policies may exacerbate this gender imbalance through policy feedback mechanisms whereby policies teach people where they stand in relationship to power influencing their own political efficacy (Lay 2019). As Kenney (1996) suggests, the gendered enactment of sexual harassment within legislatures "reinscribe(s) notions of gender that lead to women's subordination rather than liberation."

Despite the repeated conceptual expansion of what constitutes workplace sexual harassment, legal gaps still remain. Certain categories of workers, such as those who work at small businesses with fewer than fifteen employees, employees of religious organizations, people who work for tax-exempt nonprofits, and those who work as independent contractors or freelancers are not protected under current sexual harassment law and have no legal redress for harassment (Raghu and Suriani 2017). The size of the business for which the plaintiff works also determines the amount of compensatory and punitive damages, which means that two identical victims could receive differing amounts of compensation (Raghu and Suriani 2017). Discrimination policy has increasingly fallen under the purview of the courts and the bureaucracy, not the legislature. Consequently, enforcement agencies are vulnerable to pressure from the executive branch to enforce or not certain statutes on the basis of the president's preference (Nackenoff 2019). The prominence of the courts in determining what is and is not sexual harassment and what punishments should be delivered has had other negative effects.

Sexual harassment training, which was until recently supported and promoted by the EEOC, may be ineffective and used primarily by employers as a shield against liability and damages relating to harassment litigation (Bisom-Rapp 2018). In some cases, harassment training may have backfired because courts "accept these symbolic structures as relevant evidence on whether discrimination took place" (Bisom-Rapp 2018). The 1998 Supreme Court decisions in *Burlington Industries v. Ellerth* and *Faragher v. City of Boca Raton* established that an employer is legally responsible for a supervisor who harasses his subordinates but did not clarify employer liability in hostile environment cases (Bisom-Rapp 2018). These protections were weakened by the 2013 *Vance v. Ball State University* ruling that narrowed the definition of supervisor harassment to include only supervisors who have control over hiring and firing, regardless of the fact that supervisors of day-to-day work still maintain enormous power over their subordinates (Raghu and Suriani 2017). The 1999 Supreme Court case *Kolstad v. American Dental Association* ruled that employers who "engage in good-faith compliance efforts should not be assessed punitive damages," meaning, in effect, that employers can point to their sexual harassment policies and training as proof that they have done their due diligence and therefore avoid paying a settlement (Bisom-Rapp 2018). The existence of these structures also protects employers from being sued under Title VII.

Multiple studies have found that, in addition to being used mainly as a legal shield for employers, current sexual harassment policies and anti-harassment trainings are largely ineffectual and, in some cases, counterproductive (Miller 2017; Tippett 2018a). Experimental data have shown that exposure to sexual harassment policy "activates more male-advantaged gender beliefs" (Tinkler, Li, and Mollborn 2007). Other research shows that men who identify more strongly with socialized gender roles were more tolerant of harassment and that training helped participants to identify sexual harassment but did not change their attitudes toward it (Kearney, Rochlen, and King 2004). In many cases, "the law on the books often promises more than the law in action can actually deliver" in terms of workplace sexual harassment (Marshall 2005). The gap between what is theoretically due and what actually occurs is due to: lack of employee knowledge of sexual harassment policies, supervisors discouraging complaints, institutional skepticism toward complaints, fear of reprisals, the narrow understanding of what constitutes sexual harassment, and the failure of internal grievance resolution procedures (Miller 2017; Marshall 2005).

Better methods of deterring and punishing sexual harassment have been proposed. Bystander training, wherein a third party steps in to de-escalate a situation, confront a harasser after the fact, or support the victim, has been shown to be effective. Another tactic is civility training, which facilitates a healthier work environment that values everyone's contributions (Miller 2017). The EEOC recommends that new and different approaches to training, like these, be integrated into current anti-harassment workshops (National Sexual Violence Research Center 2017). Sexual harassment training should be individualized, interactive, and experiential with opportunities for feedback and practice; and its importance should be explained in order to deal with differing pretraining attitudes. Once training is complete, it should be periodically maintained through refresher courses and making adherence to the training a factor in promotions. The efficacy of sexual harassment training should be measured through posttraining attitude surveys, posttraining sexual harassment knowledge surveys, peer evaluations, and sexual harassment reporting (Perry, Kulik, and Field 2009). Monroe (2019) lists goals for reforms for universities that may be applicable to other workplaces, which should: ensure due process, protect privacy, apply censure equally to all individuals, ensure punishment is proportional to the crime, clarify reporting mechanisms, make the process transparent, create a process for publishing the results of investigations, and make public who conducts the investigations and makes the decisions. These and other reforms are difficult to implement because policies reinforce power structures and create rival interest groups that, once entrenched, can be difficult to shift (Lay 2019).

Sexual Harassment Policy in the States

State legislatures form the policy-making arm of the intermediate level of American government under the federalist system. Each state except Nebraska has a bicameral legislative system consisting of a larger lower house and a smaller upper house, wherein citizens of a state elect representatives for fixed terms. Since the 1950s, many states legislatures have undergone the process of professionalization: legislators serve for multiple terms, salaries have increased, legislatures meet more frequently and for longer periods, and legislators are supported by teams of professional staff (Engel 1999). State legislatures have enormous power to influence nearly every aspect of the lives of their constituents through constitutional amendments, taxes, welfare policies, infrastructure, criminalization of actions, business policy, and occupational licenses, among other initiatives. State government in general is also a large employer in many states, meaning that, in addition to setting workplace policy, they are themselves a model of workplace norms (Norwood 2018). States vary in how they manage this employer role, with each branch of government setting its own human resources policies in many instances (Selden, Ingraham, and Jacobson 2001).

The National Conference of State Legislatures (NCSL) was established in 1975 as a nonpartisan, nongovernmental organization to "support, defend, and strengthen state legislatures" (National Conference of State Legislatures undated). The organization also publishes a journal regarding policy innovations and professional development of state legislators and their staffs. In 2017, the NCSL published guidelines for sexual harassment in state legislatures and reviewed existing laws. According to an NCSL survey conducted 2016, 37 out of 44 state legislatures polled have "formal, written personnel policy or guidance for legislative employees" regarding sexual harassment (Griffin 2017). Our work updates this data in the wake of the #MeToo movement.

We began collecting data on legislative policies by surveying state legislative websites for public postings of their policy. If none was available, we then contacted clerks for both chambers for any information. Finally, if these routes proved fruitless, we surveyed news reports of harassment in those state legislatures for the names of those staff or legislators who were involved in calling out harassment or reforming policies. Thinking they would be the most likely to respond and have access to the policies, we emailed these specific individuals in certain states to obtain policies.

For each of the 50 states, we determined whether lower and upper chambers were covered by a singular or a joint policy. We were able to obtain 50 policies covering 64 chambers in 40 states.[4] Of the ten states with missing policies, the proportion of women ranges from 37.2% in Rhode Island to 21.5% in Oklahoma in 2019. While most of them are Republican states, Illinois and Rhode Island are not. These states do not seem to have any obvious connections as they are in all regions and all levels of professionalism. Of the 35 chambers for which we could not obtain a policy, we know that 8 of them have one, as we learned of a policy revision in those chambers through media reports. Our attempts may not have reached the right staffer and/or reflect a general unresponsiveness of bureaucracies for these states. Whatever the explanation, it is concerning that policies in these states are not available to the public, and more disturbing, of course, if they are not available to the members and legislative staffs themselves. Lack of access to a policy would prohibit victims from participating in the process to receive an appropriate response. Michigan, in particular, responded to our initial request, indicating that releasing their policy would violate the House Information Access policy, meaning that insiders have access while members of the general public do not. While at least members have access to this policy, the general public should know the standards to which their elected officials are being held.

We also found that 45 chambers had revised their policy since 2017, when #MeToo went viral.[5] Alabama's House, Maine, Mississippi's House, New Hampshire, and Tennessee are those that have not updated since fall of 2017.[6] Of the states for which a revision date for the policy was available, 12 were responding to a specific incident of sexual harassment documented in the media indicating the importance of the #MeToo movement's mission to give voice to victims. Additionally, #MeToo created a political opportunity for reformers (McCammon et al. 2001). The states with revised policies ranged across percentages of women in office, indicating critical mass is not necessary for a prioritization of this issue—particularly in a charged environment.

We then read and coded these policies to determine if the chamber policy contained the recommended characteristics suggested by the NCSL. These totals can be seen in table 8.1. In total, we examined 50 policies covering 64 chambers in 40 states.[7] These guidelines included: (1) a clear definition of sexual harassment (92% of the examined policies), (2) examples of inappropriate behaviors (76%), (3) coverage of legislators, staff, and nonemployees (77%), (4) diversity of contacts to report to (96%), (5) a clear statement prohibiting retaliation (100%), (6) a confidentiality statement (96%), (7) specific examples of potential discipline (68%), (8) the possibility of outside parties to be involved in an investigation (54%), (9) an appeals procedure (24%), and (10) a statement informing victims of their right to report to EEOC and/or the state's human rights commission (50%). Of the 50 policies, the average total score out of 10 was 7.33. Twenty-two policies were above that average while 28 fell below that. Southern states in particular fell toward the bottom of the list. Of these states, the only "above average" policy is that of the Florida Senate. The rest are below average. The South is home to the legislatures with the two lowest scores (North Carolina and Tennessee). Of the policies we had from them (10), the average score for the southern states is 6.1, which is 1.23 points below the national average.

For example, Alabama's House of Representatives specifically considers sexual harassment to consist of: "(a) Making unwelcome sexual advances or requests for sexual favors or other verbal or physical conduct of

Table 8.1 National Conference of State Legislatures' Recommended Components by State

	Clear Definition	Examples	Applicable Groups	Reporting Contacts	Prohibits Retaliation	Confidentiality Statement	Discipline Examples	Outside Investigators	Appeal Procedure	EEOC Info	Total
AK	x	x	x*	x	x	x	x	x	x		9
AL	x	x	x	x	x	x	x				7
AZ House	x			x	x	x	x				5
AZ Senate	x	x	x	x	x	x	x	x		x	9
CA	x	x	x	x	x	x				x	7
CO	x	x	x	x	x	x	x	x		x	9
CT	x	x	x*	x	x	x	x	x	x	x	10
DE	x		x*	x	x	x		x			6
FL Senate	x	x	x	x	x	x	x**	x			8
GA	x	x	x	x	x	x		x			7
HI House	x	x	x	x	x	x	x	x		x	9
HI Senate	x	x	x	x	x	x	x	x			8
IA Senate	x	x	x	x	x	x		x	x	x	9
ID	x	x	x	x	x	x	x	x			8
IN	x			x	x	x		x			5
KS	x		x*	x	x	x	x**				6
LA	x	x	x*	x	x	x				x	7
MA Senate	x	x	x*		x	x	x			x	7
MD	x	x	x	x	x	x	x		x		8
ME	x	x	x	x	x		x**			x	7
MN	x	x	x	x	x	x	x	x		x	9
MO House	x	x	x	x	x	x	x	x		x	9

MS House	x		x	x	x	x	x					6
MT	x	x	x	x	x	x	x	x		x		9
NC	x		x*	x	x				x			4
ND	x	x	x	x	x	x	x	x				7
NE	x	x	x*	x	x	x	x**	x	x	x		10
NH	x	x	x	x	x	x	x**					7
NJ	x	x	x	x	x	x	x	x	x	x		10
NM	x	x	x	x	x	x	x	x	x	x		10
NV	x	x	x	x	x	x	x			x		6
NY Assembly	x	x	x	x	x	x	x**	x	x	x		10
NY Senate	x	x	x	x	x	x	x**	x	x	x		9
OR	x	x	x*	x	x	x	x**	x				8
SC House			x	x	x	x	x**	x				6
SD	x	x	x*	x	x	x	x**	x		x		7
TN	x	x	x*	x	x	x						5
UT	x	x	x	x	x	x	x					6
VT	x	x	x	x	x	x	x	x		x		9
WA House	x	x	x	x	x	x	x	x		x		9
WA Senate			x	x	x	x	x		x	x		7
WI House	x	x	x	x	x	x	x**					7
WI Senate	x	x		x	x	x	x					6
WV House	x	x	x	x	x	x	x			x		7
WY	x	x	x	x	x	x	x					6
Total	92%	76%	80%	96%	100%	96%	68%	54%	24%	50%	12%	

* Members and staff are covered but not nonemployees.

** Only disciplinary action outlined is to dismiss.

a sexual nature as a condition of employment or continued employment. (b) Making submissions to or rejections of the conduct the basis for administrative decisions affecting employment. (c) Creating an intimidating, hostile, or offensive working environment by the conduct." The policy also includes examples of inappropriate behaviors like, "jokes of a sexual nature . . . leering . . . Touching a person's body, hair, or clothing or standing too close to, brushing up against, or cornering a person" (Alabama House of Representatives 2015). But of all ten characteristics recommended by NCSL, Alabama's House and Senate policies both contain seven in total. They lack the possibility of involving outside parties in investigations, an appeal procedure, and a statement informing victims of their ability to complain to the EEOC or the state's Human Rights Commission.

An example of the coverage component is illustrated in Hawaii's State Senate policy, which protects a broad range of subjects, including "members and staff members, as well as between supervisors and subordinates of the Senate, or vendors or lobbyists" ("2015–2016 Administrative and Financial Manual of the Senate" 2015). This type of coverage is important because of the various types of employees and supervisors to whom these subjects report, some outside the legislature itself. Of the forty policies that cover members and staff, ten do not extend that coverage to nonemployees, potentially leaving lobbyists, contract workers, and others exposed to discrimination.

An appeals process may be both good and bad. Having an opportunity to appeal a decision is important but may allow for less transparent retraction of accountability. The Maryland Assembly appeals process allows for a party involved in the reported incident to appeal to the appropriate presiding officer within ten days of receiving notice about resolution of the complaint if the party is not satisfied (Maryland General Assembly Department of Legislative Services 2017).

Transparency about the consequences of this behavior are critical for victims as well as for enforcement authorities. Victims need to understand what they can expect if they come forward and be able to weight that decision against the remedy that may be enforced. Having a range of options to suit the severity of the case sends the message that no level of harassment is acceptable while giving authorities flexibility in meting out an appropriate level of discipline suitable to the particulars of the case. In the thirty-four policies which describe specific penalties, eight of them cite only termination as a potential outcome.

Very few policies include all ten recommended components. In fact, of those policies we examined, only Connecticut, Nebraska, New Jersey, New Mexico, and the New York Assembly (12%) had policies with all ten components included. Several states had policies in at least one chamber with at least nine of the components, including Alaska, Arizona Senate, Colorado, Hawaii, Iowa Senate, Minnesota, Missouri House, Montana, New York Senate, Vermont, and the Washington House. The states with policies toward the bottom (a score of five or below) include Arizona House, Delaware, Indiana, North Carolina, South Carolina, and Tennessee.[8]

We determined that the definitions (92%), diversity of contacts to report to (96%), retaliation bans (100%), and confidentiality (96%) guidelines were most likely to be included. In fact, almost all of the policies include these components. An appeals process was least likely to be included (24%). Lastly, those states with the most guidelines covered had higher levels of professionalism, with the exception of Vermont. The states with the most covered components ranged in the proportions of women in office. No southern states had policies including nine or more recommended characteristics. We caution against any generalizations from these findings, as they are incomplete and represent only a snapshot in time. It is clear from the media coverage of these institutions that these policies remain in flux in many states.

We determined that legal guidelines which protected the institution from liability were most likely to be included, while the option for outside investigators, a statement of victims' rights, and an appeals process were least likely to be included. Further, we found that most states revised their policies in 2017–18 in response to harassment scandals in their ranks, indicating that #MeToo has had an effect. Lastly, those states with the most guidelines covered were those with higher professionalism scores, suggesting that structural features are important for worker protections.

Why Legislatures' Response to Sexual Harassment Matters

#MeToo's impact on state legislatures is obvious with seventy-six legislators accused since 2017 in thirty states (Lieb 2018). Sexual harassment policies are one response to this gender discrimination, so examining their characteristics and their ability to shape these institutions is vital to women's ability to serve in office effectively and for our own understanding of the critical ways in which gender continues to shape policymaking bodies. Having a policy in place, however, does not ensure its enforcement; and not just any policy will do. While victims emboldened by heightened attention to the issue may seize the opportunity to push for change, legislative leaders may be incentivized to ignore this problem to preserve the institution and its hierarchies. Institutions are self-protective, which benefits harassers (Lay 2019). In her examination of sexual harassment policies within universities, Lay indicates that even these minimum benchmarks for harassment policies can be problematic in intended and unintended ways.

Compliance-based systems including mandatory training may backfire, enabling sexual harassment to flourish (Chappell and Bowes-Sperry 2015; Feldblum and Lipnic 2016; O'Leary-Kelly and Bowes-Sperry 2001). For example, even when policies are in place, the way they are implemented has serious consequences not only for the individual victims but for the status of women within the institution and their own political efficacy (Lay 2019). Many scholars suggest that our contemporary approach to sexual harassment prevention is more aligned with institutional preservation than with gender equality (Bisom-Rapp 2018; Lay 2019; Raghu and Suriani 2017). Some call for a shift from a compliance-based approach to one of "inclusion, ethics, and equity" (Lay 2019). Is such change possible in legislatures? Hinckley (1983) argues that change in legislative institutions is possible through turnover in membership and when skilled leaders are motivated to act. The Associated Press reported that thirty state legislators have resigned or been removed from their posts since #MeToo went viral in 2017, and twenty-six have lost party or committee leadership positions (Lieb 2018). The dynamics of sexual harassment are such that it may deter membership turnover by discouraging female candidates, and leaders may be much less likely to enforce new norms that threaten the status quo, particularly when, as in other industries, implicated leaders are often replaced by women (Carlsen et al. 2018).

Legislatures as representative and elected bodies have their own unique challenges in dealing with this problem. Raced and gendered institutions already restrict marginalized legislators' access to power and create hostile environments and hierarchies wherein harassers may hold the power of committee and leadership appointments, party resources for reelection, and the ability to recruit primary challengers (Hawkesworth 2019). Even legislative leaders who do not engage in harassment may be incentivized to ignore or retaliate against accusers to protect political allies or in a misguided attempt to protect the institution. For example, Former Vice President Joe Biden has been criticized for his handling of the Clarence Thomas nomination hearings which he defended as necessary to uphold the norms and values of the Senate (Dionne, Washington Post 1992).

Another feature of legislatures complicating accountability is the diversity of workers within statehouses. Lobbyists, staff, and interns whose jobs depend on their ability to please legislators may be particularly vulnerable. Relationships are currency in legislatures, making power differentials and harassment particularly salient for those negotiating policy concessions in environments where quid-pro-quo harassment is rife. For those organizations or issues predominately advocated for by women, material policy implications may result.

Similarly, political campaigns are unique workplaces with volunteers, paid staff, and candidates all working in high-pressure, time-limited conditions, sometimes without clear organizational hierarchies or human-resources procedures. On-the-job training varies from campaign to campaign, resulting in varying levels of professionalism. Even with strict rules governing separation between legislative staff time and tasks and campaign staff time and tasks, it is likely that spillage may occur with informal norms of the campaign potentially encroaching upon the legislative office.

Legislators currently hold themselves accountable for a range of behaviors through self-regulation in ethics committees. The NCSL guidelines recommend the possibility of outside investigators indicating that these bodies may be unable to police themselves and that the traditional mechanisms for norm enforcement may not be enough in some cases. How likely are legislators to be capable of self-monitoring when it comes to sexual harassment?

State legislatures must get this right. In the first place, they make the law for the rest of the state's employers, and their ability to establish useful and accountable processes indicates their capacity to regulate others. If they do not understand the intricacies of sexual harassment in their own workplace, they are unlikely to be able to adequately set standards through state law. They are also an example to other employers not only by the processes they put in place for themselves but by the message their adherence to and prioritizing of their response sends to businesses throughout their state. If legislators are able to clean up their own houses, they indicate to all employers the seriousness of sexual harassment as a form of sex discrimination.

Finally, legislatures' responses to this issue also send a message to potential candidates. With women's representation in state legislatures hovering at 29%, these institutions must communicate that they are welcoming places to work. Women remain reluctant to run for office for many reasons, including the impact it would have on their families, the burden of fundraising, and feeling unqualified to do the job (Carroll and Sanbonmatsu 2013; Elder 2008). Hostile working conditions are one obstacle to women's candidacy that legislatures can do something about directly. In 2016, the National Democratic Institute launched the #NotTheCost campaign to raise awareness about the violence waged globally against women who participate in politics as either activists, candidates, or elected officials. The campaign's title challenges the claim that politically active women must accept violence or harassment as a consequence of their engagement with politics (National Democratic Institute 2019). Female state legislators are likewise entitled to run and serve in office without threat of harassment. Staffers and lobbyists, too, need not endure harassment as a part of the job.

In October 2017, Arizona State Representative Michelle Ugenti-Rita went public with accusations of sexual harassment against several of her male colleagues in the Arizona state legislature. She declined to name said colleagues, but her accusations were serious enough to prompt policy change. The following month, the Arizona House implemented its first anti–sexual harassment policy, which includes the provision of mandatory ethics training for all members and staffers. Though a step in the right direction, that policy was not enough. By November 2017, additional claims of sexual harassment in the Arizona statehouse led to the opening of a formal investigation into the matter. Three months later, in February 2018, the probe concluded that state Rep. Don Shooter had sexually harassed at least nine women during his time in office. One of his accusers was revealed to be state Rep. Michelle Ugenti-Rita. In a decidedly affirmative vote, members of the Arizona House decided to have Shooter immediately expelled from the legislature on grounds of "dishonorable behavior" (Lein-gang 2018).

By coming forward, Rep. Ugenti-Rita created a space for more victims to make complaints, which led to Rep. Shooter's ousting. #MeToo as a public calling-out of unacceptable behavior has been characterized as transformative empathy (Rodino-Colocinco 2018), and Burke's intention at the origin of #MeToo was empowerment of victims. But the movement clearly also has legal and policy implications. As the movement grows, and details about the pervasiveness and long-lasting effects of harassment become widely acknowledged, legal scholar Elizabeth Tippett (2018b) suggests that interpretations which now favor employers may be revisited—in particular, what kind of behavior counts as severe and pervasive and what responses by employers seem reasonable. She also argues that, with the dismissal of a few high-profile harassers, the expectation of appropriate penalties will also expand. As more people come forward and penalties are enforced, the norms around what is acceptable can evolve. Removal is only one important penalty. Hersch (2018) argues that the federal cap on damages for workplace harassment disincentivizes prevention and that increasing the allowable amount is critical to motivate employers to eradicate this type of behavior. Knowing that clear, consistently enforced accountability increases a victim's likelihood to report, it is clear that the consistent application of strong and varied penalties is critical to any state legislative policy.

This Arizona example points to the need for legislatures to stay vigilant and to constantly reassess their policies and their effectiveness. Symbolic compliance (Dobbin and Kelly 2007) is not enough to eradicate discrimination and project an image of legitimacy and welcome to candidates and constituents. California, for example, has dedicated $1.5 million to tracking sexual harassment in their state government and implementing new trainings for employees, despite being a year behind schedule (Venteicher 2019). Perhaps a more radical approach is necessary to eradicate this kind of behavior from society, and such proposals are unlikely to emerge from conservative state government. However, as employers, state legislatures are obligated to provide workplaces free from discrimination. The consequences of not doing so expand beyond the borders of the institution. Being able to recruit women for state legislative office and enabling them to serve at their full potential has implications for policy and gender relations more broadly, meaning that addressing the scourge of sexual harassment inside these institutions is essential not just for women serving in office but for all of us.

Notes

1. Håkansson (2019) finds that, as women move to higher office, their experiences of harassment increase.

2. Scholars have found that female legislators are more competent than their male colleagues in a number of areas (Murray 2014; Anzia and Berry 2011; Volden, Wiseman, and Wittmer 2013).

3. Cortina and Berdahl (2008) find that less than 25% of victims choose to report their harassment to their employer or other authorities.

4. We were unable to obtain policies for the following chambers or verify that they had them through news reports of their revision: Arkansas House and Senate, Florida House, Illinois House, Kentucky Senate, Michigan House and Senate, Missouri Senate, Ohio Senate, Oklahoma House and Senate, Pennsylvania House, Rhode Island Senate, South Carolina Senate, Texas Senate, Virginia House and Senate, and West Virginia Senate. Of the ten states' chambers whose policies we could not obtain, we know the following have them as we were able to determine that they updated their policies through media reports: Illinois Senate, Iowa House, Kentucky House, Massachusetts House, Ohio House, Pennsylvania Senate, Rhode Island House, and Texas House.

5. This corroborates the Associated Press, which reported that about half of the states have updated since #MeToo (Lieb 2018).

6. Alabama's Senate revised their policy in March 2018. Maine had updated its policy, which covers both chambers, in December of 2016. Mississippi's House updated in January 2013, but its Senate has refused to adopt a policy at all. New Hampshire and Tennessee updated their policies in 2016. We have included in this total the policies we know have been revised, but which we could not access for analysis. These chambers include the Illinois Senate, Iowa House, Kentucky House, Massachusetts House, Ohio House, Pennsylvania Senate, Rhode Island House, and Texas House.

7. We did not obtain any policies for the following states: Arkansas, Illinois, Kentucky, Michigan, Ohio, Oklahoma, Pennsylvania, Rhode Island, Texas, and Virginia. Michigan's House business director responded that providing the policy would violate the House Information Access policy.

8. We are unable to explain why the chambers in Arizona would be so widely different, although in our analysis this is the only state with such a large discrepancy.

References

"2015–2016 Administrative and Financial Manual of the Senate." 2015. State of Hawaii. January 21. www.capitol.hawaii.gov/docs/AdminManual.pdf (accessed August 1, 2019).

Alabama House of Representatives. 2015. "Policy Against Sexual Harassment."
March 18. www.legislature.state.al.us/aliswww/house/ALHouse_SexualHarass
mentPolicy.pdf (accessed August 1, 2019).

Anzia, Sarah F., and Christopher R. Berry. 2011. "The Jackie (and Jill) Robinson Effect: Why Do Congresswomen Outperform Congressmen?" *American Journal of Political Science* 55 (3): 478–93.

Associated Press. 2018. "Sexual Misconduct Claims in State Legislatures since 2017." AP News, August 26. apnews.com/2ed7d10fcea14efdaf5b668cdbe450f1.

Barnes, Tiffany. 2016. *Gendering Legislative Behavior: Institutional Constraints and Collaboration.* New York: Cambridge University Press.

Bauer, Nichole M. 2015. "Emotional, Sensitive, and Unfit for Office? Gender Stereotype Activation and Support Female Candidates." *Political Psychology* 36 (6): 691–708.

Berdahl, Jennifer L. 2007a. "Harassment Based on Sex: Protecting Social Status in the Context of Gender Hierarchy." *Academy of Management Review* 32 (2): 641–58.

———. 2007b. "The Sexual Harassment of Uppity Women." PsycEXTRA Dataset.

Bisom-Rapp, Susan. 2018. "Sex Harassment Training Must Change: The Case for Legal Incentives for Transformative Education and Prevention." *Stanford Law Review Online* 71: 60.

Britton, Dana M. 2000. "The Epistemology of the Gendered Organization." *Gender & Society* 14 (3): 418–34.

Brown, Nadia E. 2014. *Sisters in the Statehouse: Black Women and Legislative Decision Making.* New York: Oxford University Press.

Carlsen, Audrey, Maya Salam, Claire Cain Miller, Denise Lu, Ash Ngu, Jugal K. Patel, and Zach Wichter. 2018. "#MeToo Brought Down 201 Powerful Men. Nearly Half of Their Replacements Are Women." *New York Times.* October 23. www.nytimes.com/interactive/2018/10/23/us/metoo-replacements.html (accessed June 15, 2019).

Carroll, Susan J., and Kira Sanbonmatsu. 2013. *More Women Can Run: Gender and Pathways to the State Legislatures.* New York: Oxford University Press.

Carroll, Susan J., and Richard L. Fox, eds. 2012. *Gender and Elections: Shaping the Future of American Politics.* New York: Cambridge University Press.

Chappell, Stacie F., and Lynn Bowes-Sperry. 2015. "Improving Organizational Responses to Sexual Harassment Using the Giving Voice to Values Approach." *Organization Management Journal* 12 (4): 236–48.

Cortina, Lilia M., and Jennifer L. Berdahl. 2008. "Sexual Harassment in Organizations: A Decade of Research in Review." *Handbook of Organizational Behavior* 1: 469–97.

Dionne, E. J. 1992. "On Once and Future Supreme Court Nominations." *Washington Post.* June 19. www.washingtonpost.com/archive/politics/1992/06/19/on

-once-and-future-supreme-court-nominations/e725894a-99ed-4efa-bf22
-180c4dfe1eea/ (accessed June 15, 2019).

Ditonto, Tessa. 2017. "A High Bar or a Double Standard? Gender, Competence, and Information in Political Campaigns." *Political Behavior* 39 (2): 301–25.

Dittmar, Kelly. 2015. *Navigating Gendered Terrain: Stereotypes and Strategy in Political Campaigns*. Philadelphia: Temple University Press.

Dobbin, Frank, and Erin L. Kelly. 2007. "How to Stop Harassment: Professional Construction of Legal Compliance in Organizations." *American Journal of Sociology* 112 (4): 1203–43.

Duerst-Lahti, Georgia. 2002. "Governing Institutions, Ideologies, and Gender: Toward the Possibility of Equal Political Representation." *Sex Roles* 47 (7–8): 371–88.

Elder, Laurel. 2008. "Whither Republican Women: The Growing Partisan Gap among Women in Congress." *The Forum* 6 (1).

Engel, Michael. 1999. *State and Local Government: Fundamentals and Perspectives*. New York: P. Lang.

Erikson, Josefina, and Cecilia Josefsson. 2018. "The Legislature as a Gendered Workplace: Exploring Members of Parliament's Experiences of Working in the Swedish Parliament." *International Political Science Review* 40 (2): 197–214.

Feldblum, Chai, and Victoria Lipnic. 2016. "Select Task Force on the Study of Harassment in the Workplace (Full Report)." Equal Employment Opportunity Commission. ncvc.dspacedirect.org/handle/20.500.11990/620.

Fitzgerald, Louise F. 1993. "Sexual Harassment: Violence against Women in the Workplace." *American Psychologist* 48 (10): 1070–76.

Garcia, Sandra E. 2017. "The Woman Who Created #MeToo Long Before Hashtags." *New York Times*, October 20.

Griffin, Jonathan. 2017. "Sexual Harassment Policies and Training in State Legislatures." *National Conference of State Legislatures* 25 (26) (2017): 1–2. www.ncsl.org/research/about-state-legislatures/sexual-harassment-policies-and-training-in-state-legislatures.aspx (accessed March 24, 2019).

Håkansson, Sandra. 2019. "Do Women Pay a Higher Price for Power? Gender Bias in Political Violence in Sweden." European Conference on Politics and Gender, Amsterdam. June.

Harris, Aisha. 2018. "She Created MeToo. Now She Wants to Move Past the Trauma." *New York Times*, October 15, 2018.

Hawkesworth, Mary. 2003. "Congressional Enactments of Race-Gender: Toward a Theory of Raced-Gendered Institutions." *American Political Science Review* 97 (4): 529–50.

———. 2019. "Visibility Politics: Theorizing Racialized Gendering, Homosociality, and the Feminicidal State." *Signs: Journal of Women in Culture & Society* 45 (2): 311–19.

Hersch, Joni. 2018. "Valuing the Risk of Workplace Sexual Harassment." *Journal of Risk and Uncertainty* 57 (2): 111–31.

Hinckley, Barbara. 1983. *Stability and Change in Congress*. 3rd ed. Harper & Row.

Kearney, Lisa K., Aaron B. Rochlen, and Eden B. King. 2004. "Male Gender Role Conflict, Sexual Harassment Tolerance, and the Efficacy of a Psychoeducative Training Program." *Psychology of Men & Masculinity* 5 (1): 72–82.

Kenney, Sally J. 1996. "New Research on Gendered Political Institutions." *Political Research Quarterly* 49 (2): 445–66.

Krook, Mona Lena. 2017. "Violence against Women in Politics." *Journal of Democracy* 28 (1): 74–88.

Lay, J. Celeste. 2019. "Policy Learning and Transformational Change: University Policies on Sexual Harassment." *Journal of Women, Politics, and Policy* 40 (1): 156–65.

Leingang, Rachel. 2018. "Rep. Shooter Sexually Harassed Women, Created Hostile Work Environment, Investigator Finds." *Arizona Capitol Times*. Blog. January 30, azcapitoltimes.com/news/2018/01/30/arizona-don-shooter-sexually-harassed-women-hostile-work-environment/.

Lieb, David. 2018. "Half of States Act as #MeToo Sexual Harassment Claims Mount." Associated Press. August 26. www.apnews.com/83caf61841a84db3bbd85648bce8fec5.

MacKinnon, Catharine A. 1979. *Sexual Harassment of Working Women: A Case of Sex Discrimination*. New Haven, CT: Yale University Press.

Mahoney, Anna. 2018. *Women Take Their Place in State Legislatures: The Creation of Women's Caucuses*. Philadelphia: Temple University Press.

Manne, Kate. 2017. *Down Girl: The Logic of Misogyny*. New York: Oxford University Press.

Marshall, Anna-Maria. 2005. "Idle Rights: Employees' Rights Consciousness and the Construction of Sexual Harassment Policies." *Law & Society Review* 39 (1): 83–123.

Maryland General Assembly Department of Legislative Services. 2017. December 12. dbm.maryland.gov/eeo/Documents/SexHarrassPolicy.pdf.

McCammon, Holly J., Karen E. Campbell, Ellen M. Granberg, and Christine Mowery. 2001. "How Movements Win: Gendered Opportunity Structures and US Women's Suffrage Movements, 1866 to 1919." *American Sociological Review* 66 (1): 49.

McLaughlin, Heather, Christopher Uggen, and Amy Blackstone. 2012. "Sexual Harassment, Workplace Authority, and the Paradox of Power." *American Sociological Review* 77 (4): 625–47.

Miller, Claire Cain. 2017. "Sexual Harassment Training Doesn't Work. But Some Things Do." *New York Times*. December 11. www.nytimes.com/2017/12/11/upshot/sexual-harassment-workplace-prevention-effective.html?_r=0 (accessed June 15, 2019).

Monroe, Kristen Renwick. 2019. "Ending Sexual Harassment: Protecting the Progress of #MeToo." *Journal of Women, Politics, and Policy* 40 (1): 131–47.

Murray, Rainbow. 2014. "Quotas for Men: Reframing Gender Quotas as a Means of Improving Representation for All." *American Political Science Review* 108 (3): 520–32.

Nackenoff, Carol. 2019. "Sexual Harassment Trajectories: Limits of (Current) Law and of the Administrative State." *Journal of Women, Politics, and Policy* 40 (1): 21–41.

National Conference of State Legislatures. Undated. "About Us." www.ncsl.org /aboutus.aspx (accessed May 7, 2019).

National Democratic Institute. 2019. www.ndi.org/not-the-cost (accessed August 1, 2019).

National Sexual Violence Resource Center. 2017. "Key Findings of the Select Task Force on the Study of Harassment in the Workplace." www.ncsl.org/Portals/1 /Documents/About_State_Legislatures/Harassment_in_the_Workplace_Task _Force_32048.pdf (accessed March 26, 2019).

Norwood, Candice. 2018. "Does #MeToo Matter? Of 19 State Candidates Facing Accusations, Only 2 Lost." November 7. *Governing Magazine.* www.governing .com/topics/politics/gov-sexual-misconduct-lawmakers-midterms-2018.html (accessed August 1, 2019).

O'Brien, Diana Z., and Jennifer M. Piscopo. 2018. "The Impact of Women in Parliament." In *The Palgrave Handbook of Women's Political Rights,* ed. Susan Franceschet, Mona Lena Krook, and Netina Tan, 53–72. London: Palgrave Macmillan.

O'Leary-Kelly, Anne M., and Lynn Bowes-Sperry. 2001. "Sexual Harassment as Unethical Behavior: The Role of Moral Intensity." *Human Resource Management Review* 11 (1–2): 73–92.

Parker, Kim. 2018. "Women in Majority-Male Workplaces Report Higher Rates of Gender Discrimination." Pew Research Center.

Perry, Elissa L., Carol T. Kulik, and Marina P. Field. 2009. "Sexual Harassment Training: Recommendations to Address Gaps Between the Practitioner and Research Literatures." *Human Resource Management* 48 (5): 817–37.

Raghu, Maya, and Joanna Suriani. 2017. "#Metoowhatnext: Strengthening Workplace Sexual Harassment Protections and Accountability." *National Women's Law Center.* nnedv.org/mdocs-posts/metoowhatnext-strengthening-workplace -sexual-harassment-protections-and-accountability-large-print/ (accessed March 24, 2019).

Rodino-Colocino, Michelle. 2018. "Me too, #MeToo: Countering Cruelty with Empathy." *Communication and Critical/Cultural Studies* 15 (1): 96–100.

Rudman, Laurie A., Corinne A. Moss-Racusin, Julie E. Phelan, and Sanne Nauts. 2012. "Status Incongruity and Backlash Effects: Defending the Gender Hierarchy Motivates Prejudice against Female Leaders." *Journal of Experimental Social Psychology* 48 (1): 165–79.

Selden, S. C., P. W. Ingraham, and W. Jacobson. 2001. "Human Resource Practices in State Government: Findings from a National Survey." *Public Administration Review* 61: 598–607.

Siegel, Reva B. 2004. "Introduction: A Short History of Sexual Harassment." In *Directions in Sexual Harassment Law,* ed. Catharane A. MacKinnon and Reva B. Siegel. New Haven, CT: Yale University Press.

Tinkler, Justine Eatenson, Yan E. Li, and Stefanie Mollborn. 2007. "Can Legal Interventions Change Beliefs? The Effect of Exposure to Sexual Harassment Policy on Men's Gender Beliefs." *Social Psychology Quarterly* 70 (4): 480–94.

Tippett, Elizabeth C. 2018a. "Harassment Trainings: A Content Analysis." *Berkeley Journal of Employment and Labor Law* 39: 481.

———. 2018b. "The Legal Implications of the MeToo Movement." *Minnesota Law Review* 103: 229.

Volden, Craig, Alan E. Wiseman, and Dana E. Wittmer. 2013. "When Are Women More Effective Lawmakers than Men?" *American Journal of Political Science* 57 (2): 326–41.

Wing, Nick. May 21, 2013. "State GOP Staffer: I Was Fired after Reporting Sexual Harassment." *Huffington Post.* www.huffpost.com/entry/kirsten-anderson-iowa _n_3314259 (accessed June 15, 2019).

CONTRIBUTORS

DAVID J. ANDERSEN is assistant professor of political science at Durham University. Andersen conducts research in the fields of political psychology, political behavior, and campaigns and elections. His specific interests are in studying how voters learn about, evaluate, and choose to support political candidates. His research has been published in the *American Journal of Political Science, Political Behavior, Journal of Experimental Political Science,* and *Political Communication.*

NICHOLE M. BAUER is assistant professor of political communication in the Department of Political Science and the Manship School of Mass Communication at Louisiana State University. Her research agenda identifies the barriers that female candidates face in running for and winning elected office. She approaches this question by investigating the role gender stereotypes play in voter evaluations of female candidates, the campaign strategies female candidates develop to overcome such biases, and how the news media cover female candidates. Her research has been published in the *Journal of Politics, Political Psychology, Political Behavior,* and *Politics, Groups, and Identities.*

ROSALYN COOPERMAN is professor of political science at the University of Mary Washington. Cooperman's research has been published in the *American Political Science Review, Journal of Politics,* and *American Politics Research.* Her research focuses on women's political candidacy and campaign finance, and elite political behavior. Cooperman has been a coprincipal investigator for the Convention Delegate Studies, a survey of Democratic and Republican party activists, since 2004. She also served as a policy expert for the 2016 Presidential Gender Watch and 2018 Gender Watch projects cosponsored by the Center for American Women in Politics and the Barbara Lee Family Foundation.

TESSA DITONTO is assistant professor of political science at Durham University. Ditonto conducts research in the areas of American political behavior, political psychology, gender and politics, and race and politics. She is especially interested in how voters learn about candidates and make decisions during political campaigns, particularly when they are asked to consider nontraditional candidates. Her research has been published in *Political Analysis, Public Opinion Quarterly, Political Psychology, Journal of Politics,* and *Political Behavior,* and she has received funding from the National Science Foundation and the Barbara Lee Family Foundation.

SYLVIA I. GONZALEZ is a PhD candidate in the Department of Political Science at Louisiana State University. Her dissertation examines the intersectional identities of political candidates, with a specific focus on Latina candidates.

MIRYA R. HOLMAN is associate professor of political science at Tulane University. She is the author of *Women in Politics in the American City* (2015) and a wide variety of academic articles, including extensive research on gender stereotypes, gender and political ambition, and legislative politics. Her current research projects include investigations of gender and children's political socialization, local appointed boards and commissions, and understanding the political consequences of the MeToo movement.

MEGHAN KEARNEY is a fourth-year undergraduate studying history and political science with a minor in economics at Tulane University. She is a member of the Tulane Newcomb Scholars program and has published in Tulane's *Women Leading Change* undergraduate journal.

DANIELLE CASAREZ LEMI is a Tower Center Fellow at the James G. Tower Center at Southern Methodist University. Her current research interests revolve around understanding how identity informs formal politics. Her work has been published in *Politics, Groups, and Identities; Du Bois Review;* and *Journal of Race, Ethnicity and Politics.* Her research has been supported by the National Science Foundation, the APSA Latino Scholarship Fund, and the Peter G. Peterson Foundation.

MARY-KATE LIZOTTE is associate professor of political science at Augusta University. Her research focuses on American political behavior with a particular interest in gender. Much of her work is concerned with the origins and implications of gender differences in public opinion. She has also published research on the gender gap in voting, political knowledge, and party identification. Her work has been published in edited volumes as well as in *Politics & Gender*; *Journal of Women, Politics, and Policy*; *Social Science Journal*; and *Journal of Conflict Resolution*. Her book *Gender Differences in Public Opinion: Values and Political Consequences* will appear in 2020.

ANNA MITCHELL MAHONEY is an administrative assistant professor of women's political leadership at Newcomb College Institute at Tulane University. In 2016, she became director of research for the institute. Mahoney's work is centered on women's representation and gendered institutions, which is explored in her book *Women Take Their Place in State Legislatures: The Creation of Women's Caucuses* (2018). She also explores legislative collaboration in several coauthored articles in *Representation, Legislative Studies Quarterly,* and *Politics & Gender.*

MONICA C. SCHNEIDER is professor of political science at Miami University in Oxford, Ohio. She studies how people apply gender and racial stereotypes to political leaders in American politics, the gender gap in political ambition, and public opinion toward policies that benefit people with disabilities. Her research has been published in *Political Psychology*; *American Politics Research*; *Journal of Women, Politics, and Policy*; *Journal of Politics, Groups, and Identities*; and *Electoral Studies.*

CARLY MEGAN SHAFFER is a junior at Tulane University. She is a Newcomb Scholar double-majoring in political science and communication.

JENNIE SWEET-CUSHMAN is associate professor of political science at Chatham University, where she also served as assistant director of the Pennsylvania Center for Women and Politics from 2013 to 2019. A former congressional campaign manager, Sweet-Cushman focuses her research on women's political ambition and political representation. She currently serves on Pittsburgh, Pennsylvania's Equal Opportunity Review Commission.

INDEX

Note: Page numbers in italic refer to figures and tables.

Colorado, 141, 169
communal goals, 36–46
community-oriented legislation, 141
competence, 116–18, 159, 174n2. *See also* effectiveness of female legislators
compromise, 142
concurrent elections, 115–28
Congress (U.S.): 116th, 71–72, 84–85, 87; voter information on candidates for, 119–20; women's PACs and, 71–87; women's representation in, 1–3, 84. *See also* candidates, female; candidates, male; Democratic female candidates; House of Representatives; legislators, female; midterm elections (2018); Republican female candidates; Senate (U.S.)
Congressional Management Foundation, 40
Connecticut, 169
Conover, Pamela Johnston, 16
Conroy, Meredith, 94
consensus building, 142, 148
conservative women's PACs, 72, 78–84
constituent service, 141–42, 148
Cook, Elizabeth Adell, 116, 117
Cook Political Report, 80, 81
cooperation, 142, 148
Cooperative Congressional Election Study (CCES): 2014 data, 103; 2016 data, 7, 116, 123
Cooperman, Rosalyn, 8, 73, 75, 81
Corbin, Becky, 146, 148
Corder, J. Kevin, 13
Cortez Masto, Catherine, 55
Cortina, Lilia M., 174n3
cosponsorship of bills, 142–43, 145, 147–48, 149
Cowell-Meyers, Kimberly, 138, 143
Crenshaw, Kimberlee, 19
Crespin, Michael H., 73
Crowder-Meyer, Melody, 35, 46, 73, 81
Cruz, Ted, 58

Daley, Mary Jo, 147, 151
Dalmage, Heather M., 59

Darcy, R., 116
Dasgupta, Nilanjana, 36
Davenport, Lauren D., 55, 58
Davids, Sharice, 2
Davidson, Margo, 147, 149
Dawson, Michael C., 56, 59
Day, Christine L., 15, 16
Dean, Madeleine, 146–47, 152–53
De Boef, Suzanna, 16, 17
Deen, Rebecca, 141
Deitz, Janna L., 73
Delaware, 169
Delli Carpini, Michael X., 118
Democratic female candidates, 2–3; campaign financing and PACs, 71–77, 77, 79–87; descriptive representation and voter choice, 56–57, 62–63; gender stereotypes and, 93–110; partisan stereotypes and, 93–110
democratic legitimacy, 34
Democratic male candidates, partisan stereotypes and, 95, 97, 101–2, 107
Democratic Party: cosponsorship of bills and, 148, 149; feminine traits associated with, 94–95, 97, 99, 101 (*see also* feminine stereotypes and traits; partisan stereotypes); gender gap in vote choice and, 5–6, 13–30; presidential nomination (2020), 7–8; voter support for female candidates in concurrent down-ballot races, 116, 121–28. *See also* partisan polarization; partisanship
descriptive representation, 34; defined, 56; multiracial female candidates and, 56–67
Diaz, Daniella, 59
Diekman, Amanda B., 36–38, 44, 46
Dionne, E. J., 171
discrimination, 140, 159, 170; laws against, 153n6; policies against, 161. *See also* sexual harassment
Ditonto, Tessa, 7, 93–95, 109, 115, 117, 121, 158
Dittmar, Kelly, 6, 13, 14, 34, 73, 158
Dobbin, Frank, 173
Dolan, Kathleen, 4, 56, 63, 94, 95, 98, 109, 116, 117, 121, 143

www.ingramcontent.com/pod-product-compliance
Lightning Source LLC
Chambersburg PA
CBHW031133270326
41929CB00011B/1609